LEAD
TO REVITALIZE!

Register This New Book

Benefits of Registering*

✓ FREE **replacements** of lost or damaged books

✓ FREE **audiobook** – *Pilgrim's Progress,* audiobook edition

✓ FREE information about new titles and other **freebies**

www.anekopress.com/new-book-registration

*See our website for requirements and limitations.

LEAD
TO REVITALIZE!

15 Practices of a Church
Revitalization Leader

KENTUCKY BAPTIST CONVENTION

ANEKO
PRESS

We love hearing from our readers. Please contact us
at www.anekopress.com/questions-comments with
any questions, comments, or suggestions.

Cover Design: Jonathan Lewis
Editors: Michelle Rayburn and Ruth Clark

Printed in the United States of America

Aneko Press

www.anekopress.com

Aneko Press, Life Sentence Publishing, and our logos are trademarks of

Life Sentence Publishing, Inc.
203 E. Birch Street
P.O. Box 652
Abbotsford, WI 54405

RELIGION / Christian Church / General

Paperback ISBN: 978-1-62245-671-0
eBook ISBN: 978-1-62245-672-7

10   9   8   7   6   5   4   3   2   1

Available where books are sold

Contents

Foreword

Kentucky Baptists have always known that we are better together. From the early days of our convention, to the widespread adoption of missions funding through the Cooperative Program, to great support of our missions-sending agencies, we know that together we can do more and better than any of us can do alone. The book you hold in your hands is one more evidence of the synergistic value of our partnerships. The contributors to this work, *Lead to Revitalize!*, are from diverse backgrounds and have a wide variety of ministry experiences. They are practitioners who have served as local church pastors, church staff members, seminary professors, denominational leaders, international missionaries, evangelists, church plant-ers, worship leaders, and more. I trust you will be blessed and encouraged by their good work, whether you serve within our Baptist organization or in the greater body of Christ. My prayer for this book is that God will use it to help churches and their leaders discover that their best days of ministry effectiveness can be in front of them and not behind them. May the Lord use *Lead to Revitalize* to that great end.

Dr. Todd Gray

Executive Director-Treasurer for Kentucky Baptist Convention

Preface

Dr. Stephen C. Rice

Nehemiah was one of the greatest, most godly leaders in the entire Word of God! We can learn much about modern-day leadership from his stellar example. When King Solomon died in 930 BC, he left the kingdom of Israel teetering on collapse. As a result, the kingdom of Israel divided.

In 722 BC, 208 years after the kingdom divided, Samaria, the capital of the Northern Kingdom, fell to the Assyrians. The Southern Kingdom hung on for another 136 years until 586 BC, when Jerusalem fell to the Babylonians. The walls of Jerusalem were utterly destroyed along with Solomon's famed temple. Many of the Jews were captured and carried off to Babylon to live in exile.

In 538 BC, Cyrus, king of Persia, defeated the Babylonians and became the new world power. In His sovereignty, God led Cyrus to allow the Jews to return to their homeland and to rebuild the temple. The books of Ezra and Nehemiah (originally on one scroll) stretch chronologically from 537 to 433 BC and recount their story.

Ezra 2 tells us that when Jewish exiles returned to their homeland, Zerubbabel led them to rebuild the temple, which was finally completed in 515 BC. But, for the next seventy years after the temple's completion, the walls and gates of Jerusalem still lay in ruins. Can you imagine how that made the Jews feel? Surely, they knew they were in jeopardy. Surely, they felt deep shame and longed for a better future.

Into this hopeless, dire situation stepped Nehemiah! Despite the rocky road (pun intended) that ensued, he led them to accomplish in fifty-two days what they had not been able to accomplish in the past seventy years. His godly leadership made all the difference!

As team leader of the Consulting & Revitalization Team at the Kentucky Baptist Convention (KBC), and as a revitalization pastor for twenty-eight years, I believe that in a church that experiences revitalization, leadership is the most important factor – but not just any type of leadership – godly leadership! Churches that experience revitalization are led by pastors who walk closely with God and lead the church in the way He instructs them to lead.

In this book, we attempt to help men become godly leaders who are equipped to lead toward church revitalization. We will be the first to tell you that we don't have all the answers, but we have discovered these revitalization truths and want to add this book to the growing church revitalization volumes. We pray that His church will be strengthened and His name will be glorified as a result.

Introduction

A Revitalization Leader

Dr. Larry J. Purcell

I n many churches today, statistics about the vast number of lost people who need Christ no longer break our hearts. But it still breaks God's heart. It's time for us to wake up the church and recapture God's heart for lost people. When churches revitalize and thrive, it brings glory to God and hope to our communities. This resource can be a great primer for a pastor or ministry team that is beginning a leadership journey toward revitalization. Harry Truman once said, "Not all readers are leaders, but all leaders are readers."[1] Leadership is both science and art. In other words, you never completely arrive, but you should seek to be on a journey of continual growth and improvement. The science of leadership is seeking to learn best practices, seeking to learn the language of leadership, and seeking a better grasp of others and self. The art is taking what you learn and moving it into your life and work. The culture, context, and different personalities are the challenges of being an effective leader. It is our hope that you can use this resource to increase your knowledge and skills as a revitalization leader.

A Revitalization Leader

What are the identifiable characteristics of a leader? What makes up the characteristics of a revitalization pastor? It is critical from the beginning that a revitalization pastor acknowledges that there is not just one set of specific skills for all situations or only one personality for being an effective leader. Looking for the magic key will be a hindrance to your development as a leader and a revitalization pastor. The authors of this book desire to help a revitalization pastor identify essential skills and practices in leading his church, and to pass those practices along to another faithful believer (see 2 Timothy 2:2).

The argument is often raised that leaders are either born or made. It is my conviction that leaders are both. First, leaders are born; then they are made. Whatever a person's leadership capacity, they can always improve. Leaders can be developed to become more effective. Researchers and authors James Kouzes and Barry Posner state that "Leadership is not some mystical quality that only a few people have and everyone else doesn't."[2] The development of the revitalization pastor as a leader includes learning to ask the right questions. Kouzes and Posner suggest asking the following question: How will I make the difference I want?

Asking such a question can begin a journey of seeking to become a better learner and leader. An effective revitalization pastor will often have self-doubts. This is a common experience that has been expressed by many of the greatest leaders in the military, government, and business. This resource can help you ask the right questions, embrace the best practices, and get past some of the self-doubts.

What is Biblical Leadership?

In *Leaders on Leadership*, George Barna expressed the sentiment that the skills of exegesis and exposition can become empty if a pastor does not know how to lead.[3] Leadership can be the missing link between a revitalized church and a dying church. Yet, biblical leadership is not just about effectiveness. If a leader focuses only on outcomes or results, they may seek a shortcut that does not reflect a biblical ethic. Biblical leadership is about clearly reflecting Christ to believers and to the lost. Ephesians 4:1 can guide a leader to a biblical ethic which is reflecting Christ in all we do. The apostle Paul writes that we are to *walk worthy of the calling you have received* (CSB).

The tasks of life are an avenue for developing our spiritual walk. All believers encounter challenges in life. The family and church are the first laboratory for developing critical leadership skills. It is made evident in Ephesians 4:12 that believers are to be equipped for works of ministry and then to edify the body of Christ by investing themselves in the areas of their giftedness. The task of being a shepherd and teacher is living and leading in a way that helps develop others so that they can clearly reflect Christ as they live out their lives in the body of Christ, His church, and His kingdom. The revitalization pastor is not just a doer but also a developer. It is critical that a revitalization pastor possesses certain skills, but he must be willing to pass those abilities on to the next generation of leaders. This was demonstrated in a study of the leadership practices of revitalization pastors in Kentucky.

In a recent study led by the Kentucky Baptist Convention Church Consulting and Revitalization Team, the following ten traits were identified in revitalization pastors:

1. Revitalization pastors lean into conflict.

2. Revitalization pastors are willing to take risks.

3. Revitalization pastors work hard on church relationships.

4. Revitalization pastors take the lead in evangelism.

5. Revitalization pastors lead with a vision.

6. Revitalization pastors demonstrate dependence on God.

7. Revitalization pastors are lifetime learners.

8. Revitalization pastors develop leaders and laborers in the church.

9. Revitalization pastors lead the church to celebrate wins.

10. Revitalization pastors lead the church to implement change.[4]

We read in the Old Testament that God called one man, Abram, and from one man would come a mighty nation of twelve tribes in Israel (Genesis 12). The Lord establishes the model for us to follow in moving from one to many. Jesus began His ministry by building a team to carry on His work after His ascension. The recent lone-ranger model of being a leader or pastor is not a biblical model and is a poor system for discipling new believers. The model of our Lord and Savior in the Gospel accounts went from 1, to 3, to 12, to 120, to 3,000, and beyond. The example of and instruction from the apostle Paul was to carry someone with him on his missionary journeys. Paul would invest in Timothy, Silas, Titus, and others. He would then challenge them to pass along what they received (see 2 Timothy 2:2). Leadership is relationship. As the leader builds relationships with others, they will build leadership skills. The ten traits identified in revitalization pastors demonstrate they are not going it alone. They are not just doers of tasks but also developers of leaders.

Great leaders have followed this model of passing along what they have received either as a parent to a child or a believer to another believer. The *Shema* (Hebrew for "hear") provides fathers instruction on the responsibility of passing along what we have received to the next generation: *Repeat them to your children. Talk about them when you sit in your house and when you walk along the road, when you lie down and when you get up* (Deuteronomy 6:7 CSB). The Lord's plan for transmitting His desires and instructions to each successive generation was by oral tradition. Although we have an enormous amount of variety in communicating today, nothing can effectively replace person to person. The home is a biblical model for developing leaders.

The passages reviewed above demonstrate that a leader and revitalization pastor is to live out his calling as a public demonstration of Christ. He must not go the journey alone but take someone with him. The act of discipling is seen as a process of evangelizing with the aim of developing others who evangelize. Our Savior provided the perfect model by the manner in which He developed His disciples – a group of common men who would be accused of turning the world upside down.

A Warning

Hero worship is a common phenomenon found in North America. From the founding of the United States of America, great leaders such as George Washington, the great commanding general of the American Revolution and the nation's first president, have been worshiped as heroes. A careful reading of history demonstrates that Washington did not go through the journey alone. Certainly, Washington carried a great burden, but many battles, much less the war, would not have been won if critical people had not fulfilled their roles. The essential role of a leader is to take the lead in the development of a strategic plan and then involve others in the execution of that plan. Leaders man be viewed as heroes since they provide vital qualities of courage, decision making, strategic thinking, team development, and a host of other traits, but hero worship can be a grave limitation because it tends to deify a person.

Admiral Chester W. Nimitz has these words of his written on the United States Marine Corps War Memorial at Arlington Cemetery in Washington, DC: "Uncommon valor was a common virtue." What was witnessed during conflicts of war were ordinary men and women who displayed uncommon courage in facing life and death. Ordinary men and women are challenged to lead at critical junctures of history. Churches with a long tradition can usually identify someone in their past who made a great impact. The images or stories of the past are critical to moving a church forward, but if someone in the past is made a deity, they can become an obstacle. The Hero of the story from which we worship, preach, and lead is our Lord and Savior Jesus the Christ.

A Challenge

Declining and plateaued churches throughout North America demand leadership. Church revitalization demands that a pastor not just manage the mess but also lead healthy changes. Kouzes and Posner have researched the subject of leadership across the globe. In *Leadership Challenge*, they report that the one quality sought by all groups of followers across cultures is hope.[5] Leaders offer a new set of eyes and ears, a new view of an existing culture, and a new hope. As you study this resource, it is our prayer that you will be challenged to ask the right questions, overcome self-doubts, and embrace the best practices on your journey to becoming an effective revitalization leader who develops other effective leaders.

Chapter 1

Depending on God

Rob Patterson

Church revitalization is a hot topic because it is such a great need in so many of our churches. Pastors called to revitalization settings are obviously grateful for the prolific writing and production of resources happening in the field. However, these resources are helpful only to the degree that they drive us toward greater dependence on the only true resource for revitalization, the Lord God Himself.

Regardless of which definition of revitalization most resonates with you, there is one constant that must never be forgotten. Revitalization ultimately is God's work, achievable only by and through His power. Therefore, whatever role God calls us to play in His work of revitalizing His church, our usability will be determined by the degree to which we are actively depending on Him.

Please note the intentionality behind the seeming oxymoron

"actively depending." Such are the paradoxes of spiritual leadership. Dependence is not expressed through passivity but, rather, through active submission. Conceptually, we know that nothing of lasting value can be accomplished unless we are abiding in Christ. Jesus explains this dynamic clearly: *I am the vine; you are the branches. Whoever abides in me and I in him, he it is that bears much fruit, for apart from me you can do nothing* (John 15:5 ESV).

Apart from Christ we can do nothing, and yet we sure try. Generation after generation of church leaders drift toward prideful self-sufficiency instead of walking in humble dependence on God. Each generation can point out the shortcomings of the previous one, but don't kid yourself. This clarity is more about hindsight than insight. Some of the criticisms of past trends in church leadership are likely misplaced. The issue may not be the core ideas behind the church-growth movement, or missional church, or "insert the name of your least favorite fad here." Instead, the real issue is that some leaders allow what could be helpful resources or ideas to become substitutes for relying wholeheartedly on God.

Will the current emphasis on church revitalization prove to be just another fad or the beginnings of genuine revival? The answer lies in the heart of the revitalization leader.

The Subtle Sin of Idolatry in Spiritual Leadership

Idolatry in the heart of a spiritual leader is seldom a conscious, single decision to put our trust in something other than Christ. Rather, it is a gradual shifting of our confidence from the Lord to the good things He has used to bless our lives. Pastors can easily see this in the hearts of their people. Programs or ministries that the Lord used to draw them closer to Him or to draw their grandchildren to saving faith can become emotionally confused with the Lord Himself. A tool in His hand becomes an idol in our hearts.

This confusion is why so many churches are in desperate need of revitalization. Jeremiah 2:13 rightly diagnoses the problem: *My people have committed two evils: they have forsaken me, the fountain of living waters, and hewed out cisterns for themselves, broken cisterns that can hold no water* (ESV). Plateaued and slowly declining churches do not see themselves as having "forsaken" the Lord. Quite the opposite; many can rightly argue that they are executing programs and ministries with greater efficiency and dedication than ever before. No one is quite sure why they are seeing less fruit. There is no awareness that our affections and confidence as a local body have possibly shifted.

Perhaps it is gentler to describe it as emotional attachment rather than full-blown idolatry. Either way, if we are not careful, any of us can find ourselves valuing and worshiping the provision of God more than the person of God. How does it happen? In celebrating what God has done for us, we fall into equating the blessings of God with the God who does the blessing.

In Numbers 21, God commanded Moses to craft a bronze serpent and to set it on a pole. Whoever looked upon the bronze serpent as Moses lifted it up would be saved from the fiery serpents that had been sent among the people as the consequence of resisting and grumbling against the leadership of God through Moses. The power was not in the bronze serpent. There was nothing magical about lifting it up on a stick. It was merely a tool God used to help the people express repentance and put all their hope for salvation in God alone.

Jesus Himself helps us understand in John 3:14-15 that the bronze serpent was meant to be a symbol that pointed to Christ. *As Moses lifted up the serpent in the wilderness, so must the Son of Man be lifted up, that whoever believes in him may have eternal life* (ESV). How shocking to find in 2 Kings 18:4 that one of the major reforms Hezekiah needed to carry out in order to help revitalize temple worship was breaking into *pieces the bronze serpent that Moses had made, for until those days the people of Israel had made offerings to it* (ESV). They were no longer bringing offerings to Him because of what it represented but, rather, because of the object itself.

Look to the pews of many churches that need revitalization and you will see the same signs of drifting that we see among God's people throughout the Old Testament. Somehow the enthusiasm with which we once celebrated the building as God's provision for reaching our community has been replaced with a zeal for preserving the building itself. At some point, following the "right processes" became more important than seeing lives changed.

The subtleness of idolatry is also why many church members are so resistant to change. How could anyone suggest that we stop doing "program A" or change the way we do "ministry B" when God clearly used that program to change a life or help someone come to Jesus? Quite honestly, a change of heart is always more important than a change of programs or methodologies. So, how does the revitalization pastor shepherd God's people to recognize that their affections and confidences have shifted to something other than the Lord? How do we lead them toward repentance and a return to putting all their hope in Christ?

Prayer As the Best Measure of Active Dependence

The only way to shepherd people to depend entirely and exclusively on Christ is to model desperate dependence in our leadership. Prayer will always be the simplest and most accurate measure of our active dependence. My leadership has been significantly impacted by the ministry of Dr. Chuck Lawless. He was among my favorite professors in seminary. Our family continued to be blessed indirectly during our time serving as missionaries in the Amazon basin as Dr. Lawless served as the coordinator of prayer strategies for the International Mission Board of the Southern Baptist Convention. He could have had no idea how profoundly my life was to be shaped by a statement he made over breakfast: "It isn't hard to measure to what degree we are trying to lead from our own strength. Just pay attention to at what point in the process your prayers become desperate."

What does the current level of desperation of your prayers reveal about where or in whom you are placing your trust? How much of your weekly sermon preparation is devoted to prayer? At what point in the process of preparing a sermon do your prayers become desperate?

Perhaps no biblical text is more frequently preached or referenced when it comes to revitalization than the rebuilding of the wall through the leadership of Nehemiah. A study of the life of Nehemiah is a case study of prayer.[1] Having fasted and prayed in brokenness for many days over the state of the exiles who had returned to Jerusalem, the Lord opened a door through

King Artaxerxes whom Nehemiah was serving as cupbearer. In Nehemiah 2:4 the king asks, *"What are you requesting?"* Now, Nehemiah had been fervently praying for over four months, but before responding, he prayed. *I prayed to the God of heaven. And I said to the king* (vv. 4-5 ESV).

Scripture does not tell us what or how he prayed. We do not know if it was a silent, "Help me, God" prayer that was prayed under his breath or a public prayer voiced for all to hear. Regardless, Nehemiah, under the inspiration of the Holy Spirit, wanted us to see the right order of things. He prayed and *then* responded. Refusing to rely on past prayers, he sought God in the moment. Can your people clearly see that same reliance in your leadership?

Daniel Henderson rightly observes, "The prayer level of a church never rises any higher than the personal example and passion of the leaders. The quantity and quality of prayer in leadership meetings is the essential indicator of the amount of prayer that will eventually arise among the congregation."[2] How much prayer is actually happening in your leadership meetings? At what point in the process do you call your people to pray? What type of prayer do you model?[3]

Prayer As the Work of Revitalization

Over the years of coaching small-group leaders and church planters, I have consistently pleaded that they not delegate prayer too quickly. In our attempts to involve people, prayer seems like an easy opportunity. However, D. A. Carson writes, "Many facets of Christian discipleship, not least prayer, are rather more effectively passed on by modeling than by formal teaching. Good praying is more easily caught than taught."[4] Obviously, we must teach on prayer, but Luke 11:1 makes it clear that it was Jesus' example of prayer that awoke within the disciples a hunger to learn how to pray more effectively.

If your people replicate in their prayer lives what they see in you, will your church be on the path to revitalization? Recognize that little more can be achieved than what is fought for in prayer. Richard Foster urges, "We need not worry that this work will take up too much of our time, for 'It takes no time, but it occupies all our time.' It is not prayer in addition to work but prayer simultaneous with work. We precede, enfold, and follow all our work with prayer."[5] Prayer is the means and measure of active dependence.

Chapter 2

Prayer and the Revitalizing Leader

Andy McDonald

Many pastors find themselves in a revitalization work with the church they serve. You may be reading this book because you are in a revitalization work. Our sincere desire as you read through these pages is that you will know there is hope for your church. This book provides coaching and advice about best practices and strategies for a successful church revitalization. And while it contains many good things a pastor might do to try to turn things around, I would argue that none is more important than prayer. In fact, prayer is the one indispensable activity for any successful revitalization effort. S. D. Gordon once said, "You can do *more* than pray, *after* you prayed, but you can *not* do more than pray *until* you have prayed."[1] It's almost a tongue twister, but his point is clear: plan to start in prayer, or plan to fail.

In John 15:5 Jesus said, *"I am the vine; you are the branches.*

The one who remains in me and I in him produces much fruit, because you can do nothing without me" (CSB). Many things could be said about what it means to remain in Christ, but He clearly tells us just how important it is because without Him we can do nothing. That's zip, zilch, nada. This certainly includes the work of revitalizing a church. In verse 7 of the same chapter, Jesus says, *"If you remain in me and my words remain in you, ask whatever you want and it will be done for you."* As we remain in Christ vitally connected to Him through prayer, we can count on Him to hear and answer our faithful requests.

Dependence on God

That leads me to the first prayer point in a revitalization effort: *Prayer reflects our absolute dependence on God's power for the work.*

I saw an illustration of this many years ago when I was serving at a church in central Kentucky as the student pastor. It was an exciting time for the church. We were in the middle of a building campaign and members watched in anticipation as a new family-life center was going up. I was excited because the students had just gone back to school and we had planned our annual back-to-school outreach event called "Sloppy Olympics." The event always drew a huge number of students.

The new construction had created an enormous pile of dirt. My plan was to use some of that dirt to create a giant mud pit for our Sloppy Olympics competition. Great plan, right? The problem was, I hadn't recruited a single person to help me move the dirt from the pile to my would-be mud pit nearby (that's a whole revitalization topic for another time). On the day of the event, it was just me and a shovel. As I began to move dirt from the pile to the designated area, it took me all of thirty seconds to figure out this was never going to work. I thought, "The students are going to arrive in a few hours and the only mud to be found is going to be attached to my name!"

But then I saw it. The answer to my problem was just a few feet away. A gleaming hunk of glorious metal called a Bobcat front-end loader. I thought, "If I had that Bobcat, I could make quick work of this job."

I didn't delay in getting to the point with Doug, the project foreman. I told him about my dilemma and then I asked, "Doug, can I borrow your Bobcat?"

He paused before asking, "Have you ever used one before?"

I told him I hadn't.

He looked at me rather incredulously and then tossed me the key and said, "Be careful."

In thirty minutes, I had all the dirt I needed for our Sloppy Olympics, and the event was saved . . . and so were some students when I presented the gospel later that evening!

The Lord taught me a valuable spiritual lesson that day. He showed me that so much more can be accomplished when I depend on His power through prayer than when I rely on my own strength alone. Simply going to the right person, Doug, and asking for the right tool, a Bobcat, turned an impossible job into a relatively easy one. I'm not suggesting that prayer will make a revitalization work easy, but I am saying that prayer moves a seemingly hopeless and impossible situation into the realm of hopeful and very possible. That day I was reminded of this truth: God can do in five seconds what human effort alone could never do in five hundred years.

One of the greatest temptations any revitalization leader will face is to forget that *unless the Lord builds a house, its builders labor over it in vain* (Psalm 127:1 CSB). The best revitalization strategy in the world won't produce a revitalized church if there's no dependence on Christ as reflected in desperate cries for His help in prayer. Before you develop a strategy, before you make a single plan, and before you recruit the first leader in a revitalization effort, bathe every bit of the work in prayer. Acknowledge that you are completely dependent on Christ and that apart from Him, you can do nothing.

What circumstances make it easy for you to depend on God? When are you most tempted to take the reins from God and do things your way? Take some time to pray and ask God to help you radically depend on Him in every aspect of the revitalization effort.

A Prayer Strategy

Praying out of our dependence on God for a revitalization work, we move to our second prayer point: *Revitalization calls for a prayer strategy.*

If you're going to see your church turn around, you need a plan that creates a culture of consistent and effective prayer. It has been said, "If you fail to plan, you are planning to fail."[2] A revitalization prayer strategy doesn't have to be complicated, but it does need to be clearly communicated and easily reproducible. Here are some practical suggestions for developing a revitalization prayer strategy.

The Pastor Leads the Way

In the Bible, whenever God prepared to do a great work, He raised up a leader. John Maxwell says, "Everything rises and falls with leadership."[3] When it comes to prayer, the pastor sets the example for members to follow. It's vital that you are meeting with the Lord daily and desperately seeking His power, wisdom, and direction for the work. When it comes to churches that are plateaued or in decline, no occasional, halfhearted prayers will do. In Acts 4:13 the Bible records: *When they observed the boldness of Peter and John and realized that they were uneducated and untrained men, they were amazed and recognized that **they had been with Jesus*** (CSB, emphasis added).

Education and training didn't make the apostles bold; it was being with Jesus that made the difference. Revitalizing a church isn't for the faint of heart, and a pastor engaged in the work may often find himself on the front lines of a spiritual battle. The only way to stay encouraged and enthusiastic for the work is by spending daily time with Jesus through a vital prayer life.

Mobilize Members to Pray

Another important aspect of a revitalization prayer strategy is to mobilize church members to pray with you. Perhaps you're thinking, "I'm not sure anyone else in this church actually prays"; after all, there's a reason the church needs revitalization. While it may be true that some members are lacking in their passion for prayer, there are likely at least a few who have a heart for prayer and would welcome your invitation to join you in prayer for revitalization. Even if only a few have a heart for prayer, don't be discouraged. Jesus only needed twelve to turn the world upside down. Here are some ideas for leading your church to join you as you pray for revitalization:

- Explain to church members why revitalization is necessary and the importance of the church joining together in prayer.

- Share with the church about your prayer life and teach your people how to pray. You're not boasting, but simply allowing your people to see your example. Jesus led by example in His own prayer life, and when His disciples asked Him to teach them how to pray, He obliged their request (see Luke 11:1-4).

- Provide a list of revitalization prayer points with corresponding Scriptures for your people. This could be a made into a simple bookmark or provided electronically via email, social media, or a daily text reminder. The list might include:

  o Pray to hunger and thirst for righteousness (see Matthew 5:6).

  o Pray for a greater desire to read, study, memorize, and obey God's Word (see Psalm 119:140).

  o Pray for repentance of sin and revival among the people of God (see 2 Chronicles 7:14).

  o Pray for a desire to see the Great Commission fulfilled in our day (see Matthew 28:19).

  o Pray for the lost by name (see Acts 26:18).

- o Pray for young families to come into the life of the church (see Acts 2:47).

- o Pray for leaders to be Spirit-filled and for new leaders to emerge (see Ephesians 5:18; 2 Timothy 2:2).

- o Pray for effective outreach efforts in the community (see Colossians 4:5).

- o Pray for strong marriages and families (see Hebrews 13:4).

- o Pray for life and vitality in the church's ongoing ministries (see 1 Corinthians 16:9).

- Saturate every worship service and Bible study with prayer. Consider inviting members to come to the altar to pray not only after the message but before as well.

- Meet with your men at nontraditional times for prayer.

- Recruit and train prayer leaders for every small group or Sunday School class.

- Train members to pray spontaneously throughout the day. If someone shares a prayer request, stop and pray for their request immediately.

- Encourage prayer partnerships or networks where members regularly pray together for the work of revitalization. Pastor, you especially need a network of church leaders who will regularly pray for you and the church.

Plan Prayer Emphases throughout the Year

One final element of a comprehensive revitalization of prayer strategy is to develop a yearly prayer calendar with special emphases on prayer taking place throughout the year.

- Once or twice a year, preach a sermon series on prayer.

- Plan a prayer retreat with a revitalization theme.

- Invite a prayer leader to come and do a special training.

- Lead your church through a season of focused prayer for revitalization. The Kentucky Baptist Convention has a helpful resource called "40 Days of Prayer."[4]

- Encourage members to sign up for online prayer tools such as BlessEveryHome.com.

- Do a door-to-door campaign, asking your neighbors how you can pray for them. This will often present gospel-sharing opportunities.

- Encourage members to set a phone alarm for 10:02 a.m. or p.m. (see Luke 10:2) to remind members to pray for workers and for the harvest.

When it comes to your prayer life, are you comfortable saying this with the apostle Paul: *Imitate me, as I also imitate Christ* (1 Corinthians 11:1 CSB)? All of us need to grow in the spiritual discipline of prayer; what's one step you could take to deepen your prayer life? Take some time and develop a rough outline of a comprehensive revitalization prayer strategy for the church where you serve.

Persevere in Prayer

In this chapter, we've explored how the revitalization leader desperately needs to depend on the Lord in prayer, and we've examined the importance of developing a strategic approach to leading the church to pray. One final revitalization prayer point is this: *The revitalizing pastor must persevere in prayer.*

Forgive me for stating the obvious, but most revitalization churches will not turn around overnight. The journey back to health and vitality may take several years. And honestly, some churches never make it back. There will be successes and setbacks and mountain peaks of excitement followed by valleys of disappointment. Some members will be your greatest cheerleaders, only later to become your biggest detractors. There will be seasons of significant gains followed by crushing losses. As I mentioned earlier, this is not for the faint of heart. And some days the only thing that will keep you going is this singular truth: the One who called you to this work is worthy of your best effort to see it through to the end. So how does one keep his hands to the plow when it would be easier to walk away?

The answer, in large measure, is to persevere in prayer. In Luke 18, Jesus gave the parable of the unrighteous judge and the persistent widow. He told the story to illustrate the *need for them to pray always and not give up* (Luke 18:1 CSB). Persevering prayer believes that God cares far more about you,

His church, and the work of revitalization than you ever will or could. Persevering prayer waits patiently but asks expectantly, believing that God is perfectly able to breathe new life into a tired church. Persevering in prayer is waking up early, walking the well-worn path to that sacred place where you meet with the Master, just you and Him. And in that holy place of prayer, the Lord gives you what you need to continue the work to which He has called you, the work of revitalization. May the words of the prophet Isaiah greatly encourage your heart:

> *I brought you from the ends of the earth*
> *and called you from its farthest corners.*
> *I said to you: You are my servant;*
> *I have chosen you; I haven't rejected you.*
> *Do not fear, for I am with you;*
> *do not be afraid, for I am your God.*
> *I will strengthen you; I will help you;*
> *I will hold on to you with my righteous right hand.*
> (Isaiah 41:9-10 CSB)

Are you struggling to persevere in prayer? Be encouraged; you're not alone in that struggle. What one step might you take today that will help you to persevere in prayer?

Chapter 3

Leading with Vision

Rob Patterson

J ust as there are many contributing factors to cardiovascular disease, there will be a combination of issues that lead to a decline in congregational health. But as evangelistic disciple making is the lifeblood of the local church, the bottom line for declining churches is declining effectiveness in reaching and making disciples locally. Strategies that help stabilize a church but fall short of mobilizing God's people to engage their as-you-are-going circles of influence might be important first steps, but they cannot lead to lasting revitalization.

The revitalization pastor needs a clear vision from God of how to lead the current generation of a local church in evangelistically making disciples in their unique community context. Every church and community is unique, so there is no one-size-fits-all plan for revitalization. Yes, there are biblical callings, identifiable competencies, and key characteristics that can be grouped into models. However, one of the reasons so many churches are in desperate need of revitalization is the tendency of trying to lead from borrowed vision. How then does a pastor discover God's unique vision for revitalization? Over the years, authors and insightful leaders have reached a consensus that God's unique vision for a local church will be found in discovering the overlap of three spheres of God's sovereign activity: clarity of calling, church's gifting, and community context.

The Clarity of Calling and the Revitalization Pastor

The story of God's people, recorded within the Bible as well as in countless histories of local churches, makes it clear that there are critical moments when God sends leaders for specific reasons. Since birth, the Lord has been using everything that has happened in a leader's life to uniquely prepare him for leading God's people in fulfilling the good works He has prepared for them to do (see Ephesians 2:10). E. M. Bounds affirms, "Men are God's method. The Church is looking for better methods; God is looking for better men."[1]

One hundred percent of the time in revitalization there is

a change of leadership. Either the church calls a new pastor, or the current pastor experiences personal revitalization. A testimony frequently heard within revitalization circles is, "God changed me. I'm not the same leader I was before."

Such renewal can be the fruit of faithfully waiting on the Lord, as revitalization is seldom seen without a serious stick-to-itiveness on the part of the pastor (see Isaiah 40:28-31; Habakkuk 2:2-4). Renewal also results from repenting from trying to lead in our own strength or overconfidently relying on past successes, competencies, or methods. Sometimes it is the fruit of remembering and returning to priorities that once were in our daily agendas but have drifted due to loss of intentionality or neglect.

Many pastors schedule retreats to plan out their preaching for upcoming months. Some schedule times for strategic planning or big-picture thinking. Both are important habits, but it is vitally important for visionary leaders to also schedule times for self-reflection. Acknowledging that organizations are prone to "mission drift" is easy. Admitting that organizational mission drift frequently begins with loss of strategic focus and intentionality in the leader can be harder.

Are you consistently giving most of yourself to what matters most in leading your church toward revitalization? Early in ministry, I prayerfully identified some clear priorities in Paul's pastoral letters to Timothy. I began blocking off time for these key actions, knowing that priorities that do not make it to our calendars will never become the rhythms of our lives. Monthly, I would take a quick inventory: How consistently am I living out what I say are God's priorities for my life and ministry? As part of an annual spiritual retreat, I reflected and listened for how God wanted to continue growing me in these "seven *E*'s." (Yes, the alliteration belies the time.)

Am I setting an *example* of what it looks like to be an authentic follower of Jesus? Is my leadership setting an example of what it looks like to live out our church's vision? Am I doing the work of an *evangelist*? Who am I *equipping* for greater kingdom impact, for exponential disciple making? Can I see evidence of how my *exhortation* is leading people to greater trust and obedience to God's Word? How often and effectively am I *encouraging* others? Am I gratefully *enduring* whatever is necessary for the sake of the elect? Am I *interceding*, committing all of this to prayer?

Okay, there are six *E*'s and one *I*. This book expresses these priorities in different terms, but isn't that the point? Diversity of personalities, life experiences, and spiritual gifting mean each pastor will live out these values differently. The uniqueness of how God is working in the life of a pastor is a key piece of the revitalization puzzle, but it is not the only piece.

The Collective Gifting of the Church

One of the greatest mistakes a pastor can make in accepting the call to a church is believing the lie that he will be bringing Jesus in the U-Haul. God has been at work in that church long before you arrived and, in many cases, long before you were even born! The revitalization pastor is characterized by a profound appreciation for the legacy of God's work through His people in this place.

When a pastor arrives with a set of predetermined changes

already in mind, it can have more to do with pastoral preferences than leading toward God's preferred future. That truth merits repeating. Leading from your preferences will not always result in leading to God's preferred future. Caution! Personal preferences can become idols just as easily in the pulpit as in the pew.

Instead of arriving with assumptions based on what worked somewhere else in the past, the better questions might be: Where is God working in the church right now? How has God worked here in the past?

It is hard to find clarity of where God is leading without carefully considering the trajectory of the past. Will Mancini argues that as we better understand the history and "vision that has gone before, we pull back the slingshot for our own."[2] Invest significant time in listening to the shared stories of the church. Appropriately celebrating how God has moved in the past is vital to inspiring the church to embrace what God is calling them to do next.

The collective gifting and passions of the church is another way to discern how God desires to work through a church for His glory. When teaching on spiritual gifts, Paul makes this affirmation: *God arranged the members in the body, each one of them, as he chose* (1 Corinthians 12:18 ESV). If the gifts needed for launching methods or programs are simply missing, who's really missing them? The first step toward pastoring the church of your dreams is loving the church you have. The resources come from the harvest, but the harvest comes from equipping and mobilizing the actual people in the church to live missionally in their local community.

The Current Community Context

The frustrating reality for many churches is that they are perfectly designed to reach the community of twenty or more years ago. What good is it to offer the best version of an outdated program or provide a service that nobody cares about anymore? Good missiological and church-planting principles remind us that the gospel message must be contextualized, which is an ongoing process. While the gospel is universal and unchanging, every community is unique and constantly changing.

Poor or outdated contextualization results in the gospel being rejected as "foreign" or irrelevant. A good missionary friend once observed, "The problem with many of our approaches to evangelism and church planting is that we show up with rehearsed answers to questions no one is actually asking." How well do we know the people we are called to reach? Do we know the questions they are asking?

You will not find them in a demographic study or in a committee meeting. The only way to contextualize the gospel is to get out into the community and into the lives of people. The more a pastor is involved in personal evangelism, the more effective he will become in preaching evangelistically, because real-life conversations and questions will be in the back of his mind as he studies the text.

Where good demographic studies are helpful is in identifying who really lives within a one- to three-mile radius of the church. How much do those inside the church resemble those living around the church? If a person living next door visits on Sunday, would they easily be able to see themselves fitting in? Does reaching the current community seem more like cross-cultural missions? What will it take for the current generation of your church to make disciples in your neighborhood?

The reason many churches struggle to gain traction is that their revitalization models are based on what they see in regional churches, when God's design is for them to be a neighborhood church. Regional models can be hard to scale to normative-size churches and often may not fit the culture of your local community. Regardless, how can one affirm the sovereign intentionality of God and then behave as though the physical address of the church is not a vital part of His plan?

The first step toward pastoring the church of your dreams is loving the church you have. The first step toward regional impact is making a difference on your own street. If most members have migrated out of the community as the community has changed over the years, would some be willing to move back in for the sake of Christ? If large multi-housing developments are being built, who would consider moving into one with a missionary mindset? How can our facility become a community resource?

Revitalization is dependent upon helping the church reconnect to the founding dream. At some point in the past, a group of believers looked at your community and said, "They need Jesus. They need a church that looks like them and can reach them for Christ." Returning to that original dream provides the vision for revitalization.

A Compelling Picture

Every New Testament church, including those in decline, knows that their mission is to fulfill the Great Commission. What is missing for most is a clear, compelling picture of what it looks like for the current generation of the church to make reproducing disciples in their changing community context. That vision can be discovered at the nexus point of these three overlapping spheres of God's sovereign activity: clarity of calling, church's gifting, and community context. The calling of the revitalization pastor is to provide a living, compelling picture of how a changed life can be used to change lives, a church, and a community.

Chapter 4

Preaching to Revitalize

Alan Dodson

Over many centuries and from many cultures, there is a proverb that encourages the hearer not to overlook what should be obvious. Here's my favorite version of "For Want of a Nail," a proverb that has taken on many variations:

> For want of a nail, the shoe was lost.
> For want of a shoe, the horse was lost.
> For want of a horse, the rider was lost.
> For want of a rider, the battle was lost.
> For want of the battle, the kingdom was lost.
> Everything was lost for want of a horseshoe nail.[1]

Failing to think about what should be obvious can have terrible consequences.

You have many resources as a revitalization leader. From

instruments to assess current reality to exercises aiding a vision and ministry alignment process, revitalization resources are abundant and accessible. As you formulate your revitalization strategy, do not forget to think about and pray through how you should levy your greatest asset – the one God has chosen to use as perhaps the most powerful means to move and shape His people. Prepare yourself to preach toward revitalization.

Preach the Word

It was AD 64, and the maniacal Emperor Nero ruled Rome. On the nineteenth of July, a fire broke out in the merchant shops near Circus Maximus, ancient Rome's sprawling chariot stadium. Nine days later, two-thirds of the great city lay in ruin. Someone had to be blamed, and under the burden of speculation himself, Nero targeted the Christian community. So began the great Roman persecution of the early church. Nero mercilessly persecuted Christians. He indiscriminately crucified them. "During gladiator matches he would feed Christians to lions, and he often lit his garden parties with the burning carcasses of Christian human torches."[2]

Christianity's first great missionary and theologian was not immune to the persecution. In AD 67, the apostle Paul finds himself in a dank Roman prison awaiting his execution. Days before his beheading, the Holy Spirit inspired him to write his final letter to his protégé Timothy. It had been four years since Timothy received his first letter from Paul. Ministry was difficult, and the church at Ephesus needed revitalization.

Throughout the letter, the trustworthiness and sufficiency

of Scripture are underscored. Consider the constant, unmistakable emphasis on the Word of God in each chapter of 2 Timothy (CSB):

Don't be ashamed of the testimony about our Lord. (1:8)

Hold on to the pattern of sound teaching that you have heard from me. (1:13)

What you have heard from me in the presence of many witnesses, commit to faithful men who will be able to teach others also. (2:2)

Correctly [teach] the word of truth. (2:15)

All Scripture is inspired by God and is profitable for teaching, for rebuking, for correcting, for training in righteousness, so that the man of God may be complete, equipped for every good work. (3:16-17)

The strongest encouragement for the pastor to make full use of the Word of God in his ministry comes from the final chapter of the letter:

Preach the word; be ready in season and out of season; correct, rebuke, and encourage with great patience and teaching. (2 Timothy 4:2 CSB)

Here, Paul encourages Timothy first of all to keep the Word central in his ministry of exhortation. If the Ephesian church would experience revitalization, it would be the result of responding to proclamation. In preaching the Word, Timothy would present God as the church's hero, not himself.

Second, Paul challenged Timothy to preach the Word at all times. The words *in season and out of season* tell us that the revitalization pastor should preach the Word when it is easy and when it is difficult. He should preach it when the fruit is evident and when the fruit seems invisible. His trust doesn't lie in his abilities to proclaim the Word or the congregation's readiness to receive it, but in the power of God's Word to accomplish its purpose. *My word that comes from my mouth will not return to me empty, but it will accomplish what I please and will prosper in what I send it to do* (Isaiah 55:11 CSB).

When a congregation receives constant nourishment from Scripture, it will bear into their lives, and the church will be strengthened. The Word will *rebuke*. The Word will *confront* the hearer with his sin. The Word will *correct*. The Word will not only confront the hearer with his sin, it will also *turn* him toward the right way. Finally, the Word will *encourage*. The Word will support, comfort, and aid the hearer. A pastor who leads in a revitalization effort must commit himself to preaching the Word. Dry bones live when the Word is proclaimed (see Ezekiel 37).

The Preacher As Elder, Overseer, and Shepherd

The revitalization pastor must remember who he is as he preaches. There are three terms used interchangeably in the New Testament, each describing a facet of a pastor's work. If he is to lead toward change, he must not abdicate his biblical responsibilities during the event when the majority of the congregation sees and hears him – preaching the sermon.

These terms are most clearly used describing the same person – the pastor – by the apostle Peter. *I exhort the elders among you as a fellow elder and witness to the sufferings of Christ, as well as one who shares in the glory about to be revealed: Shepherd God's flock among you, not overseeing out of compulsion but willingly, as God would have you; not out of greed for money but eagerly; not lording it over those entrusted to you, but being examples to the flock* (1 Peter 5:1-3 CSB). In these verses, Peter, himself an *elder*, writes to *elders*. He encourages them to *shepherd* and *oversee* their churches.

The apostle Paul also uses the same terms describing the work of the same person. *Now from Miletus, he sent to Ephesus and summoned the elders of the church. Be on guard for yourselves and for all the flock of which the Holy Spirit has appointed you as overseers, to shepherd the church of God, which he purchased with his own blood* (Acts 20:17, 28 CSB). Paul calls together *elders*, acknowledges their calling as *overseers*, and challenges them to *shepherd* their congregations.

The biblical, three-fold ministry of the officer we most commonly refer to as pastor is that of serving as elder, shepherd and overseer. John MacArthur states, "Each term describes a different facet of the same office." He explains that *elder* refers to spiritual maturity, *shepherd* refers to nurturing the flock, and *overseer* refers to leadership.[3]

The term *elder* simply speaks of the maturity and wisdom that an older person should have, which makes them qualified for leadership. In its application, it is more about wisdom and maturity than a specific age. It isn't the number of candles on a man's birthday cake that qualifies him as an elder. It's the spiritual maturity wrought in his life through the work of the Holy Spirit over a journey of discipleship.

A *shepherd* is one who tends his flock. Perhaps, in evangelical churches, it conjures up our favorite image for the person who leads a New Testament church. We favor the term *pastor*, which is derived from the Latin term for "shepherd." A spiritual shepherd does his job in two primary ways. First, he feeds the sheep. A pastor spiritually feeds his congregation as he exposits the Word of God. Second, he tends the sheep, which, among other things, means leading them.

An *overseer*, or bishop, directs and administrates the affairs of the church. A New Testament church was never meant to be run by committees. It is to be led by a bishop. As a good leader, he communicates current reality, describes the preferred future of the church, and articulates the path to pursue that vision.

Realizing that the pulpit is the primary place where the majority of the congregation sees and hears their pastor, a revitalization pastor leads from the pulpit as elder, overseer, and shepherd. As *elder*, preach as one who has walked with God. Acknowledge your need of the Word. Don't sharply separate your sermon preparation and devotional life. Rather, apply the Word to yourself first. The congregation will more fully receive the challenge to change when they see that the sermon that is delivered to them has been applied by the deliverer.

As *overseer*, preach as one who understands the congregation, has a vision of a preferred future, and has a willingness to lead the congregation to pursue it. In your sermons, help the congregation face reality. The people deserve and want to know how things stand with the church. A good leader defines reality and at the same time describes a preferred future.

Revitalization preaching should inspire the congregation by showing them an attainable destination. But getting there requires change. Preach boldly to challenge the people and effect change. Congregations must be challenged to press toward life change.

As their *shepherd*, preach to your parishioners as one who loves them and wants what is best for them. There are three connectors that bridge the visionary overseer and the caring shepherd: hope, trust, and love. The revitalization pastor must be a merchant of hope who delivers that commodity from the pulpit. As a shepherd, explain how our hope of living out what Christ asks of us resides in the power of the Holy Spirit.

Shepherds intentionally cultivate trust. A primary way to do that from the pulpit is by the use of transparency. In the pulpit, be open and honest as a person. Let your sheep see their shepherd as a real person, not someone who pretends to be a spiritual superhero. When you make a misstep in leadership, let them know. When you are elated by advancement, let them see your excitement. Sheep won't let you lead them if they don't trust you, and they won't trust you if your preaching ministry is built on pretense.

Shepherds love their people and put their own agendas second to the people they lead. A wise pastor will tell his people every Sunday, in one way or another, how much he loves them.

Preach Revitalization Content, Especially Repentance

The revitalization pastor must be aware of what Scripture says about revitalization and preach it. Scripture is replete with revitalization themes. Here are some of them:[4]

- Nehemiah is a handbook for leading a revitalization project, speaking to every revitalization issue, including prayer, vision, brokenness, confession of sin, organizational leadership, spiritual leadership, communication, opposition, obstacles, and renewal.

- Ezekiel has a vision of dry bones – they live when the Word is proclaimed.

- Haggai's message is of returning to that which God has called us.

- The admonition of Jesus in the garden of Gethsemane speaks to prayerlessness.

- In Acts, Paul's second and third missionary journeys illustrate the need to strengthen existing churches.

- Ephesians calls us to love, just as Jesus taught.

- Galatians addresses errant theology that leads to church problems.

- The books of 1 and 2 Corinthians address specific issues in the fellowship of the church, including theological issues, ecclesiological issues, and moral issues.

- Jude urges believers to contend for their faith, reject immorality, and submit to spiritual authorities.

- Hebrews offers encouragement for those who are about to give up.

- The letters to the churches in Revelation expose the current realities of the churches and call them to repentance.

The one theme you cannot overlook as a revitalization pastor is repentance. True church revitalization is precipitated by revival, and revival is the fruit of repentance. A church will not experience true spiritual revitalization until it recognizes its sin and repents.

To preach repentance, you must understand what it is. True repentance is more than just returning to God. It's returning to Him with a broken, contrite heart. Listen to the words of the prophet Joel: *"Even now—this is the LORD's declaration—turn to me with all your heart, with fasting, weeping, and mourning. Tear your hearts, not just your clothes, and return to the LORD your God"* (Joel 2:12-13 CSB). David wrote Psalm 51, detailing his journey of repentance following his sinful escapade. He stated, *The sacrifice pleasing to God is a broken spirit. You will not despise a broken and humbled heart, God* (Psalm 51:17 CSB). We obtain a broken heart when we grasp the relational aspect of sin. Sin isn't merely a failure of performance; it is also a breakdown in intimacy with God. That's why David stated, *Against you—you alone—I have sinned* (Psalm 51:4 CSB).

Pastor, do not fail to understand and preach repentance. Most often, a weak church is weak because of sin. It could be corporate issues such as complacency, selfishness, apathy, or lack of evangelism. Perhaps immorality in personal lives is rampant among the members. Boldly call the church to repent. Without revival, true spiritual revitalization will elude your people, and revival will never come without repentance.

Chapter 5

Evangelizing to Revitalize

Dr. Kenny Rager

I was supposed to be happy about this church in the neighboring town, but I was not. The church was growing, and they were seeing many people saved. Some reports said that fifty people were saved in one month. They had quickly become the talk of all the neighboring communities. I should have rejoiced, but instead I was disheartened.

Don't get me wrong; I was genuinely thankful that people were saved at this other church. Still, I was discouraged that my own church wasn't seeing as many salvations. This was the first church I had ever pastored, and it was located in a small town with a fleeting population. The church had little money, little technology, and low education. We were blessed with several middle and high school kids who would attend on Wednesday nights, but the kids were unruly, unengaged, and disrespectful.

We would never have the resources that the other church had, but God would still use our church to reach the lost.

God taught me several lessons at this church (one being that I should never compare my church to another church). God would show me that He can use any church to reach the lost. He can use churches with resources, and He can use churches without resources.

You may feel that your church is lacking the programs, money, and resources needed to evangelize the community. You may even be afraid to reach new people for fear they will see the "mess" and you will be embarrassed. The temptation may be to think that you will revitalize the church first and then begin to reach the lost, but this is rarely the case.

Should My Church Really Evangelize?

Jesus was clear that we are to participate in the Great Commission (see Matthew 28:18-20). We need to be reminded that these words were a commission and not a suggestion. The first church took the commission seriously. Notice Peter, the bigmouthed representative of a ragtag band of disciples, in the second chapter of Acts. Peter concludes his Pentecost sermon with these words: *"Repent, and let every one of you be baptized in the name of Jesus Christ"* (Acts 2:38 NKJV). After the Spirit came, they were equipped to effectively share the gospel of Jesus Christ.

The first church had few resources. They lacked facilities, training programs, freedom, and developed leadership. They didn't even get deacons until the church grew to several thousand (see Acts 6). The first church lacked much but still had all they needed. They had an abundance of Holy Spirit power and boldness. Regardless of what your church is lacking, your church still has access to the same Holy Spirit who gives us the courage to witness.

When a person is saved, they become "born again" (John 3:3). Have you ever noticed what happens when a young couple brings home a baby from the hospital? They are often met with various forms of celebration such as visits from family and friends, balloons on the mailbox, or a stork sign in the yard. New life brings joy. When people are saved and baptized in your church, they will carry joy with them. The church will begin to see the power of God and will be encouraged. An encouraged congregation is critical for the revitalizing pastor.

In addition to joy, new believers also bring unique gifts and talents into the body. Maybe your church lacks skilled musicians. What if some of those you evangelize are musicians who accept Christ and eventually become worship leaders? Just as babies change the dynamics of a household, new believers will change the dynamics of a church.

You don't have to wait for things to be better before you evangelize. Actually, you shouldn't wait at all. Instead, you ought to evangelize to revitalize. Don't worry about a lack of money, a lack of people, or even internal church problems. Use what God has given you and share the good news with others.

Door-to-Door Evangelism

God has placed your church right where it needs to be. Paul said, *[God] has determined their preappointed times and the boundaries of their dwellings* (Acts 17:26 NKJV). Trace the history of your church and discover the reason the church was planted.

Likely you will find that it was planted to reach the surrounding neighborhood. God wants this church in this community. Unless He has told you to relocate the church entirely, you must focus on reaching your area for Christ.

Door-to-door evangelism is a great way to begin evangelizing your community. Sadly, I often hear people say, "Door-to-door evangelism is no longer effective." I would like to challenge this line of thought. Not only do I believe door-to-door evangelism is valid, but I also believe your church should be doing it. Regardless of your church's financial resources, door-to-door evangelism is an excellent way to engage your community with the gospel. All you need are houses, gospel tracts, and your Bible.

First, define the goal of door-to-door evangelism. If your goal is to proclaim the gospel of Jesus Christ faithfully, then you will be a success every time you present the gospel at the door. If the person accepts Jesus, you praise God. If all you can do is give the gospel, praise God. If you are polite, respectful, and courteous, and a door is still slammed in your face, then praise God. You attempted to share the gospel.

Use gospel tracts when going door to door. I recommend utilizing a tract with large print, pictures, and a full presentation of the gospel. Follow these simple steps:

1. Knock on the door, take three steps back, and wait for someone to answer.

2. When someone comes to the door, hand him or her the tract, introduce yourself, and share that you are out visiting the community.

3

3. Transition the conversation by asking, "Do you have any spiritual beliefs?"

4. Ask if you can read the tract to them. If they agree, then share the good news of Jesus.

5. At the conclusion, ask if the person is ready to receive Christ. If they desire salvation, then lead them in a prayer to receive Jesus. If they are not ready, ask if you can pray for them and if you can come back later.

Even if your church is located in a sparsely populated community, there are still houses near the church. By going to these homes and presenting the gospel, you will faithfully evangelize. The community will also be introduced to the pastor and will become more familiar with the church. I have had great success with door-to-door evangelism, and I have even had some pray to receive Christ. Those who prayed to receive Christ at the door had no problem with me coming to their house. They thanked me.

Identifying the Lost

God has placed your church where it needs to be, and He has also put certain people in the lives of your church members. The first chapter of John gives more details about the calling of the first disciples. The text states that Jesus finds Philip, and then Philip finds Nathanael. Philip proceeds to tell Nathanael that he has indeed found the Messiah (see John 1:43-51). Evangelism is often conducted through a relationship with a lost friend or family member.

Oscar Thompson's classic book *Concentric Circles of Concern* helps the Christian identify specific lost people within their social networks. For a more in-depth study of relational evangelism, I would recommend Thompson's book to be read and then taught in your church. For the sake of this chapter, let's look at how to utilize Acts 1:8 to help identify the lost in the lives of your church members.

Acts 1:8 says, *"You shall receive power when the Holy Spirit has come upon you; and you shall be witnesses to Me in Jerusalem, and in all Judea and Samaria, and to the end of the earth"* (NKJV).

This passage is often used to help churches think about missions in geographic terms. "Jerusalem" is the hometown. "Judea" may be the county or state. "Samaria" is the nation, and "the end of the earth" is the foreign mission field. Though this is a great way to apply Acts 1:8 for missions, it may also be adapted to relational evangelism. Think of the geographic locations of Acts 1:8 in terms of relationships.

- Jerusalem = Lost family

- Judea = Lost friends

- Samaria = Lost neighbors and coworkers

- The end of the earth = Lost acquaintances (servers, bank tellers, clerks, others with whom you may cross paths)

After teaching your people how to identify the lost, you can then have them write those names or relationships on a piece of paper. When the lost have been identified and recorded, each person can now place the list in their Bible or display it somewhere as a reminder. After the congregation identifies the lost, the pastor should lead the congregation to begin praying for these people and then train the congregation in how to share the gospel with them.

By helping your people identify the lost in their lives, you will help them make a transition into obedience. Remember, not everyone has been taught to think of evangelism in these terms. The straightforward act of identifying the lost may ignite passion and fire in the hearts of your people. Fire and passion for the lost will do much to help revitalize a congregation.

Big Days

I love the parable of the great banquet (see Luke 14:16-24). The master has invited several people to a banquet, but those who were invited did not come. So then he tells his servants to *"Go out into the highways and hedges, and compel them to come in, that my house may be filled"* (Luke 14:23 NKJV). The parable encourages us to go out and compel people to come in.

"Big day" evangelism is one way we can encourage people to come in and hear the gospel. A big day can be Easter, Mother's/ Father's Day, the beginning of a revival meeting, or any type of special meeting. Friends and family days have proven to be greatly beneficial for reaching the lost. The idea is to set aside a special Sunday morning that doesn't compete with church or community activities. The church is encouraged to invite their lost friends and family to attend.

Big days do require some preparation but don't have to be costly. First, make sure you set a day and start planning toward it early; don't spring it on your people. You want to make sure your people have plenty of time to think and pray about who they are going to invite. Second, set a goal for your big day (have some faith and encourage people to meet the goal). Third, give invitations to your people to invite their lost friends and family. Remind them that these invitations are for people who need to receive encouragement to come. Finally, on the big day, preach the gospel and give an invitation to receive Christ. The big day isn't the best day to pull out your tithing sermon. Instead, you need to have a well-planned worship service that presents the gospel and calls for the lost to make a decision.

A final word about big days. Make sure you collect contact information from the guests who attend. I would recommend you have everyone fill out a connection card and place it in an offering plate. After receiving the information, make sure you follow up. Send a handwritten note, make a phone call, or go visit them. Even though some did not make a decision on the big day, it doesn't mean that God isn't working on them. You will need to follow up.

Can My Church Really Make a Difference?

You may feel there are just too many obstacles and too many internal problems to evangelize. You may also argue that there isn't enough money. The three ideas above challenge these mindsets. They cost little to nothing to conduct, they require few volunteers, and they work. They may create much-needed momentum for your revitalization efforts.

The neighboring church I mentioned at the beginning of this chapter did reach several people for the Lord. That same year, our small church didn't reach half as many, but we did reach one. His name was Marty, and Marty was part of that unruly youth group that met on Wednesday nights. Many thought Marty was beyond hope, but our church kept working with him. We eventually saw Marty give his life to Christ.

Unfortunately, years later, Marty passed away at an early age. I'm not sure if we set the woods on fire with evangelism, but I do believe we made a difference, even if it was only the difference in one life – the life of Marty. Your church can make a difference too, even if it's in the life of only one person.

Chapter 6

Discipling to Revitalize

Rick Howerton

Disciple making is the key to revitalizing a church. A disciple church will never need to be revitalized again in the future. Why? When a church is primarily made up of spiritually mature Christ-followers, that church is never void of leaders who make decisions based on God's kingdom agenda. These churches have much less conflict than most churches because spiritually mature Christians exhibit *love, joy, peace, patience, kindness, goodness, faithfulness, gentleness, and self-control* (Galatians 5:22-23 CSB). These churches consistently keep the best interests of others in mind, pray more, evangelize more, serve more, give more, are on mission more, and embrace biblical principles and rationally motivated change more than churches that aren't made up of and led by mature disciples of Jesus Christ.

Spiritually mature people have advancing God's kingdom

as their primary goal. Their hearts have been reshaped to love like Jesus loves, serve like Jesus serves, think like Jesus thinks, care for others like Jesus cares for others, and sacrifice their own wants and wishes, even their own lives for the church as Jesus gave His life for the church. If the church you're revitalizing has been on a downward trajectory due to lack of trust among the church membership, lack of passion for the kingdom of God, lack of evangelism, lack of focus on mission, lack of willingness to sacrifice for the cause of Christ, or lack of concern for the community where the church exists, it most likely created its own reality due to its lack of disciple making.

Spiritually immature people have their own agendas in mind. Because their hearts haven't been reshaped through sanctification, they struggle to discern God's will for themselves and for the church God has placed them in. Paul wrote to the church in Rome, *Do not be conformed to this world, but be transformed by the renewing of your mind, that you may prove what is that good and acceptable and perfect will of God* (Romans 12:2 NKJV). As people are discipled to maturity, their minds are renewed, and their renewed minds become more and more aligned with the mind of Christ.

The first letter to the church in Corinth, 1 Corinthians, was written to a church made up of spiritually immature people. Due to this fact, they experienced the following in their church:

1. Divisions (see 1:10)

2. Sub-Jesus heroes (see 1:12)

3. Refusal to accept the truths of God's Word, which deemed them foolish (see 2:14)

4. Jealousy and strife (see 3:3)

5. Holding to worldly ideals (see 3:18-19)

6. Arrogance (see 4:6)

7. Sexual immorality (see 5:1)

8. Hesitancy to exercise spiritual discipline (see 5:9)

9. Unfaithfulness in marriage (see 7:1-5)

10. Putting personal appetites before the spiritual needs of the spiritually immature (see 8:13)

11. Idolatry (see 10:7)

12. Grumbling (see 10:10)

13. Social-class snobbery (see 11:17-34)

14. Spiritual-gift snobbery (see 12:1-14:40)

15. Not recognizing the authority of their church leaders (see 16:15-18)

Go back and read that list slowly. If you know the history of the church you've been called to revitalize, you'll most likely find that many of these issues characterize or have characterized the church as it began on and continued on a downward trajectory. What happened? Spiritually immature leaders made decisions based on personal agendas and the agendas of those they longed to please. Evangelism became a secondary consideration as the church's programs became a higher priority than lost souls. When conflict occurred, rather than practicing principles from Matthew 18, those involved were more determined to win the fight than keep the unity of the body of Christ, and those who were unable or unwilling to stomach such childishness left the church. And the list could go on and on. The bottom line is this: a church primarily made up of spiritually mature people – people who exhibit the characteristics of Christ – will create a healthy, whole, Christlike, and gospel-focused church.

The last directive Jesus gave His disciples was: *"Go therefore and make disciples of all the nations, baptizing them in the name of the Father and of the Son and of the Holy Spirit, teaching them to observe all things that I have commanded you; and lo, I am with you always, even to the end of the age."* Amen (Matthew 28:19-20 NKJV). Jesus didn't say go and gather church members or go and enlist class members, He said go and *make disciples*. Disciple making is the key component to rebuilding a broken church.

What Does Making Disciples Mean?

Disciple making is twofold: (1) evangelizing the lost – *baptizing them* (Matthew 28:19); and (2) discipling believers to high levels of maturity – *teaching them to observe all things that I have commanded you* (Matthew 28:20). It's important to realize that Jesus placed both of these expectations in one statement. Discipleship and evangelism are not two independent and separate ministries in the local church. Mature disciples evangelize. Let me say that again. Mature disciples evangelize.

In order to understand how and why these two responsibilities are a package deal, we must understand the process by which Jesus discipled. Jesus is our model for disciple making. We must know how He discipled so that we can do what He did. At least sixteen times in the Gospels, Jesus is called "Rabbi."

Every rabbi had his disciples. The goal of every disciple of a given rabbi was to see his disciples become imitators of the rabbi who was discipling them. Rabbi Jesus longed to see those under His tutelage imitate the way He lived. He wanted them to pray like He prayed, teach what He taught, teach the way He taught them, serve the poor as they had seen Him serve the poor, heal as He healed, and live out their relationship with God the way Jesus lived out His relationship with His heavenly Father. In Luke 6, Jesus reminds His disciples, *"Everyone who is perfectly trained will be like his teacher"* (Luke 6:40 NKJV).

The learning process was much different than is ours today. When Jesus called His disciples, He declared, *"Follow me"* (Matthew 4:19). This wasn't a call to be involved in a seminar or attend a class Jesus was teaching. In our current world when we think of someone teaching, we envision a room with a whiteboard up front, a professor espousing information that students are to write down on paper or type into their computer, and when the class bell rings, everyone leaves for their next lecture. There's no personal relationship between teacher and student. The teacher's primary goal is to unearth information to be regurgitated for future use – in most instances a written exam – meaning a personal relationship with the teacher is unnecessary.

In Jesus' day, because the disciples were learning to live the lifestyle of their rabbi, they literally followed their rabbi around. An ancient Jewish saying stated that if you chose to follow a rabbi, you should "cover yourself in the dust of his feet and drink in his words thirstily."[1] The students were so often with and so close to their rabbi that they were covered with the dust stirred up by the rabbi's feet as he walked ahead of them on the road.

Disciple Making Is Relational

Biblical disciple making is relational. It's inviting someone or a few others to allow you to be their discipler. They agree to learn to become like Christ as you lead them. Because disciple making is relational, it's imperative that you choose to disciple no more than three other people at a time. A group larger than this will keep you from giving the time and attention necessary to make mature disciples. As their discipler, you carry out a threefold responsibility: model, mentor, and meet.

Model. Modeling Christlikeness is one of a disciple maker's primary responsibilities. Like Paul, if we have journeyed with Christ long enough and have been discipled ourselves, we are able to say, *"Imitate me, just as I also imitate Christ"* (1 Corinthians 11:1 NKJV). Don't let this expectation be too daunting. If you're discipling someone, you're most likely further along in the transformational journey than they are. Being one step ahead of those you're discipling is enough.

Mentor. You mentor those you're discipling as you teach them specific skills of a maturing Christ-follower. Some of those skills include

- how to have a daily quiet time, a life-changing time with God each day;

- how to be a witness for Christ;

- how to pray;

- how to study the Bible; and

- how to resolve conflict with someone else.

In order to teach important skills, use a five-stage process.

1. Model the action for those you are discipling.

2. Ask them to do what they've seen done.

3. Follow up by encouraging them in what they did right and reveal what they still need to work on.

4. Have them do that which still needs work until they get it right.

5. Set them free to do what they now know how to do.

Meet. It's essential that you meet weekly with those you're discipling and that your weekly gathering be all it needs to be. This begins with choosing the right curriculum. Curriculums vary in their approach to the weekly meeting. However, all disciple-making gatherings should include the following experiences:

- Prayer

- Accountability for assignments made the week prior

- Scripture study and discussion

- A time for the disciple maker to respond to questions from those they're discipling

- Assignments/homework to be completed by the next meeting

These are some tremendous curriculum options for discipling:

- NavPress – 2:7 Series

- discipleFIRST – Grow Series

- LifeWay – Disciples Path Series

Disciple Making Is Generational

Paul told young Pastor Timothy, *The things that you have heard from me among many witnesses, commit these to faithful men who will be able to teach others also* (2 Timothy 2:2 NKJV). In order for disciple making to transform lives as well as a church, someone disciples some, who disciple some, who disciple some, and so forth. The greatest growth is experienced not when someone has been discipled but, rather, when the person who has been discipled is discipling someone else.

When you recruit those you're going to disciple, be sure to make them aware that your goal is for them to make disciples as well. When your journey with them has ended, they will then recruit a new group of three to disciple. By doing this, you not only grow disciples and strengthen your church, you also set an example for those you've discipled. They will do what they have seen done by the one who discipled them, not what they've been told they're supposed to do.

Someone once wisely said that you can't consider yourself a disciple maker until you've discipled someone (Paul's Timothy), who has discipled someone (Timothy's witnesses), who has discipled someone else (the witnesses' faithful men), who has discipled someone else (the faithful men's others). This is a true statement.

Disciple from the Top Down

When Paul speaks of *faithful men* in 2 Timothy 2:2, I believe he's talking about those who are already in leadership. In most churches, this would be elders, deacons, and staff members. This is top-down discipleship, that is, discipling those in leadership who have agreed to disciple others who agree to disciple others. When a pastor has a group of influencers who are willing to be discipled first, he establishes that spiritual matters are more important than material matters, that relationships are more important than programs, and that God's Word is more important than the church's governing documents.

A wise revitalization pastor will follow the disciple-making strategy depicted in the following diagram where you (the pastor) will disciple *faithful men* (deacons or elders) who disciple others (non-leader laymen).

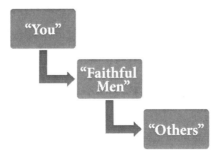

Imagine a Church

Imagine a church where the pastor is surrounded by spiritually mature men and women who are willing to sacrifice all for the kingdom of God. Imagine a church never void of leaders. Imagine a church where decisions are made based on the Word of God. Imagine a church where church members embrace the role of the lead pastor and follow his leadership without ongoing questioning. Imagine a church where church members share the gospel and invite others to church services weekly so they can hear the gospel presented. Imagine a church where the majority give a tithe and there's enough income to meet every need.

In order for what you're imagining right now to become a reality, you must disciple a few, who disciple a few, who disciple a few, who disciple a few, with this sequence continuing over and over again.

Please allow me to repeat what I said at the very beginning of this chapter: Disciple making is the key to revitalizing a church. A discipled church will never need to be revitalized again in the future. Why? When a church is primarily made up of spiritually mature Christ-followers, that church is never void of leaders who make decisions based on God's kingdom agenda. These churches have much less conflict than most churches because spiritually mature Christians exhibit *love, joy, peace, patience, kindness, goodness, faithfulness, gentleness, and self-control* (Galatians 5:22-23 CSB). These churches consistently keep the best interests of others in mind, and they pray more, evangelize more, serve more, give more, are on mission more, and embrace biblical principles and rationally motivated change more than churches that aren't made up of and led by mature disciples of Jesus Christ.

Now, let's go make disciples!

Chapter 7

Developing Leaders

Rick Howerton

L eadership development is an essential element of church revitalization. In order for a church to come back to life, it needs leaders who are passionate about the mission of the local church. And what is the mission of every biblical church? Jesus Himself gave it to us: *"Go therefore and make disciples of all the nations, baptizing them in the name of the Father and of the Son and of the Holy Spirit, teaching them to observe all things that I have commanded you; and lo, I am with you always, even to the end of the age." Amen* (Matthew 28:19-20 NKJV). In order for a church to come back to life, it needs leaders who know, understand, promote, and live the vision of the church. In order for a church to meet the needs of its congregants, it needs leaders to lead teams of people who meet one another's needs. In order for a church to reach critical mass and continue in a pattern of ongoing growth, the church needs multiple leaders at work guiding the congregation to join them as they accomplish the mission and vision of the church.

One of the roles of all pastors, especially revitalization pastors, is given to us by God Himself. Paul tells us in Ephesians 4:11-12 that *He Himself gave some to be apostles, some prophets, some evangelists, and some pastors and teachers, for the equipping of the saints for the work of ministry, for the edifying of the body of Christ* (NKJV). Every revitalization pastor is responsible for finding, recruiting, and equipping leaders.

Disciple First-Tier Leaders

Before we dive into the waters of leadership development, let's land on the right and effective path to leadership. The following diagram depicts the stereotypical church's path to leadership where evangelism progresses to membership, which progresses to leadership.

When this is the pathway leading to leadership, spiritually immature leaders are given authority. Leaders going directly from salvation to membership to leadership is the downfall of many churches. In fact, if you're revitalizing a church now, look back at the church's history. You may find that this was what created the downward trajectory. Due to the fact that spiritually immature people are often unable to focus on the needs of the church and the kingdom more than their own wants and wishes, or the wants and wishes of those who have their ear, spiritually immature leaders are apt to make decisions based on the longings of the vocal minority, the person to whom they're married, or something they read on the latest blog post.

Spiritually immature leaders are less likely to see what God's Word has to say about an issue because the spiritually immature aren't biblically knowledgeable. Spiritually immature leaders are less likely to pray about a decision because they aren't in the habit of an ongoing prayer life. When things don't go their way, spiritually immature leaders lean toward winning the ideological or methodological war more than keeping unity in the body of Christ. They are apt to build a small coalition to vote their way so they can get their way. Oftentimes, this leads to disunity in the church body and may lead to a church split.

It's imperative that a person be discipled before they are put into a substantial leadership role. The next diagram depicts the biblical route to leadership where evangelism progresses to discipleship, which progresses to leadership.

In 1 Timothy, Paul unearths the qualifications of those who are to be placed in primary leadership roles. In most churches, either the qualifications for deacons or the qualifications for pastors and elders are required of those who serve in substantial leadership roles. As you read the following passages, take note that only those who are at high levels of spiritual maturity will meet the biblical standard.

Qualifications of Pastors and Elders

This is a faithful saying: If a man desires the position of a bishop, he desires a good work. A bishop then must be blameless, the husband of one wife, temperate, sober-minded, of good behavior, hospitable, able to teach; not given to wine, not violent, not greedy for money, but gentle, not quarrelsome, not covetous; one who rules his own house well, having his children in submission with all reverence (for if a man does not know how to rule his own house, how will he take care of the church of God?); not a novice, lest being puffed up with pride he fall into the same condemnation as the devil. Moreover he must have a good testimony among those who are outside, lest he fall into reproach and the snare of the devil.
(1 Timothy 3:1-7 NKJV)

Qualifications of Deacons

Likewise deacons must be reverent, not double-tongued, not given to much wine, not greedy for money, holding the mystery of the faith with a pure conscience. But let these also first be tested; then let them serve as deacons, being found blameless. Likewise, their wives must be reverent, not slanderers, temperate, faithful in all things. Let deacons be the husbands of one wife, ruling their children and their own houses well. For those who have served well as deacons obtain for themselves a good standing and great boldness in the faith which is in Christ Jesus. (1 Timothy 3:8-13 NKJV)

Recruiting First- and Second-Tier Leaders

My personal definition of leadership is: *The ability to obtain and retain followers, organize them, unify them, and direct them to accomplish a God-given vision.* As a revitalization pastor, you must embrace the fact that leadership begins with a God-given vision. The mission of the local church was established by Jesus Himself when He told His church to *make disciples* (Matthew 28:19). But the vision the pastor pursues will vary from pastor to pastor. For instance, some pastors are called to make disciples through a program-driven church, others by being a cell church, and still others by using a simple-church model. Vision is what great leaders use to obtain and retain followers.

Never forget that leadership is relational. Through the building of relationships, a revitalization pastor earns the right to share the vision he has been given and is then effective in inviting those with whom he's in relationship to join him in working together to make the vision a reality. When recruiting leaders, look for people who exhibit the following characteristics:

- Humility (see John 13:1-17)

- Influence (see Luke 2:52)

- Wisdom (see James 3:17)

- God-given communication skills (see Jeremiah 1:9)

- Teachability (see Proverbs 9:9)

These types of future heroes are much more apt to be effective leaders than those who lack in these areas. As you recruit leaders, also look for four qualities:

1. Character

2. Chemistry

3. Competency

4. Capacity

Someone lacking *character* will, at some point, cause much pain for the pastor or will force the pastor to be involved in time-consuming cleanup. Since you'll be working with these individuals for many hours, when possible, choose those with whom you have *chemistry*. While these two characteristics are essential, *competency* must be high on the list. If they are incapable of accomplishing the work, they will be of no use to you or the team they lead. Finally, be certain the leaders you recruit have the *capacity* in their schedule to establish character, exhibit chemistry, and prove they are competent. If there's someone you're considering for a leadership-development pathway but the time they have available keeps them from all that is involved, they will become frustrated, and you will be disappointed in them.

Developing Future Leaders

If you're going to develop leaders, you must have a strategy you lean into. Due to emotional intensity and the time required of a revitalization pastor, it would be wise to utilize the following seven practices.

As you read

Every great leader is also a great learner. This means you'll be reading books, blog posts, articles, and so forth. Each time you come across content that will aid in the development of your future and present leaders, email or text the link to the article or blog. Make them aware of great leadership books. Let them know that when you get together with them, you'll discuss the reading together.

As you listen

Most great leaders listen to podcasts and sometimes listen to audiobooks. When you come across a great podcast or book, send the link to the people you're equipping. It's amazing how much leadership wisdom and knowledge can be gained in a twenty-minute podcast or by listening to a leadership book while driving, exercising, etc... The following are some excellent leadership podcasts to consider:

- Craig Groeschel Leadership Podcast

- Church Leadership Podcast by Watermark Church

- Carey Nieuwhof Leadership Podcast

As you watch

The amount of leadership training that is available free on YouTube.com and other sites online is unfathomable. Each time you come across a great video, let the people you're preparing for leadership know where it's located and what the content is about. Even more importantly, ask them to let you know when they come across a great leadership video. Few things are more encouraging to someone in the equipping phase of leadership than realizing they have given something of value to the person who mentors them, something that aids in the mentor's growth as well.

As you go
Those who develop great leaders do what Jesus did with His twelve: they ask those in training to be with them and not just sit in classes they teach. If you lead a meeting, take a leader in training with you. If you visit someone in the hospital, take a future leader with you. If you're involved in a difficult conversation, take someone who is becoming equipped with you. If you lead a strategic planning session, ask a future leader to listen and learn.

In your circles
One of the most effective ways for future leaders to learn leadership principles and practices is by meeting in "book circles" – a group of six or fewer led by the revitalization pastor. Each week, attendees are required to read one chapter of a leadership book. The revitalization pastor then leads a discussion based on the content of the week's chapter. The following are some great options for leadership books:

- *Developing the Leader Within You* by John Maxwell

- *Spiritual Leadership* by Henry Blackaby and Richard Blackaby

- *The Way of the Shepherd* by Dr. Kevin Leman and William Pentak

- *Start with Why* by Simon Sinek
- *Lincoln on Leadership* by Donald T. Phillips

When you conference
When attending a conference, always take as many leaders in training with you as possible. You'll find that these overnight or day-trip experiences bond the group, establish you as their leader, create conversations at meals and after sessions that are eye-opening and transformational, and aid you in realizing when someone is and isn't ready to take on a significant leadership role.

As you mentor
Mentoring is more than all that is noted above. Mentoring moments are those times when you are teaching a specific skill. This could be goal setting, strategic planning, creating job descriptions, recruiting volunteers, hosting a pre-event meeting, and so on. When mentoring, it's wise to use a five-step process.

- Step 1: I do, you watch.
- Step 2: You do, I watch.
- Step 3: I encourage you for what you did well, followed by sharing what you need to work on.
- Step 4: You try again until you get it right.
- Step 5: I set you free to do it on your own.

Empowering Leaders
When the time comes when you believe those whom you have

been developing as leaders are ready to lead, it's important that you empower them for leadership. This should be done ceremonially as well as on an ongoing basis. It would be wise to allow the congregation to be part of a ceremonial experience. Since the leaders you've been raising up will be leading within the context of the congregation, they will be given instant respect and will be seen as leaders the moment you ceremonially bless them; in doing so, you will establish them as leaders.

On an ongoing basis, privately, progressively, and consistently encourage those who are your leaders. Throughout the Bible, we are told to build one another up and to encourage one another. On a private level, when you see your leaders doing something right, anything, tell them. When leaders you've raised up continue to grow in their leadership, remind them of how far they've come and that you've noticed how much more they have to offer at present. Consistently, at every opportunity, point out how God is using their leadership to make a difference in the church and in the lives of those they lead. By so doing, your leaders will remain in the game over the long haul, continue to grow as leaders, and be able and willing to develop leaders in the way you developed them.

Chapter 8

Growing through Groups

Darryl Wilson

In John 10:11, Jesus identifies Himself as *the good shepherd.* The sheep in our care belong to Him. That elevates the importance of our job. In fact, Jesus says that our job of caring for each other will show the world our love for Him. *"I give you a new command: Love one another. Just as I have loved you, you are also to love one another. By this everyone will know that you are my disciples, if you love one another"* (John 13:34-35 CSB).

If we are not faithful in caring for the sheep God has given us, why should He send us more? Sunday School and small groups help the pastor and church care, disciple, and mobilize His sheep well. This chapter will take a practical look at five key actions that lead revitalization churches toward effective care of the sheep through groups.

Enlisting more shepherds

In my experience, a teacher or small-group leader can only care well for about five people. That means more shepherds are needed to provide more care. Enlisting new leaders is also an effective way of increasing discipleship and involvement. Every group will benefit from the addition of two shepherds who point the group toward care.

The *member-care leader* will lead group members to

- develop a member-care list,

- contact every absentee every week,

- plan and conduct a fellowship event and a project every quarter,

- mobilize care for members in need, and

- keep good attendance and contact records.

The *prospect-care leader* will lead the group to

- develop a prospect-care list,

- make consistent and caring contact with prospects at least every other week,

- invite prospects to fellowships and projects, and

- welcome and seek to enroll prospects who attend the group.

For a group to grow beyond five members, both member and prospect leaders are needed. Group members will serve in these two roles in both youth and adult groups. In preschool and children's groups, two of the teachers will serve in these roles.

With the addition of these two leaders, the group will be able to provide care for ten to fifteen people.

Enlistment always begins with prayer. In Matthew 9:38, Jesus reminds us that we are to *pray to the Lord of the harvest to send out workers into his harvest* (CSB). After praying, we open our eyes, observe those around us, ask them to help us, and watch what God is doing in and through them. When He leads us to someone, we tell that person of our prayers and observation and invite him or her to join us in doing the important work of care. Each new leader needs training and ongoing coaching in order to be effective.

Caring for the sheep in the sheep pens
Consistent, caring contact matters. When a group member is absent, the group should notice and respond with care. If the member misses three times, absence may become a habit, making it more difficult to return. In response, the member-care leader assigns members to contact absentees every week that they are out. Because care matters, the member-care leader follows up by asking how the contacts went.

Contact is made in a variety of ways – visits, phone calls, mail, and electronically. The most personal contacts are often visits and calls, but asking members about their preferred method of connection may make communication even more effective. Caring contacts will often include these elements: telling members they were missed without producing guilt, following up on a previous prayer request, reminding them about an upcoming fellowship or project, asking for prayer requests, and praying together.

When needs are discovered, the member who makes the contact shares the information with the member-care leader. The member-care leader then leads the group to plan and take steps to mobilize care. Needs can involve childcare, financial assistance, transportation, grief care, and much more.

Fellowship events and projects are additional ways of strengthening the Velcro of caring relationships. Fellowships tend to be more social, and projects tend to involve more work. Because both help members (and prospects) get to know one another better in different ways, it's effective to plan one of each type quarterly. Extend intentional invitations to all members (including absentees) and prospects. Planning for these fellowship events and projects will often be led by the member and prospect-care leaders but will include many group members.

Adding more sheep pens

In my context, adding a new sheep pen (group) tends to increase attendance by about ten people each week within twelve to eighteen months. This should come as no surprise, since a new group will add new leaders who can provide more care for more people. It is also true that new people are often more open to joining a new group than a previously existing one. And leaders and members of new groups tend to invite people more often.

Consider these eight steps for adding a new sheep pen (group):

1. Pray and follow God's lead.

2. Identify and enlist the leadership team and provide training.

3. Determine when and where the group will meet.

4. Set the launch date and communicate it in advance.

5. Obtain the needed resources.

6. Invite the target audience.

7. Launch and celebrate the start.

8. Continue to encourage and coach the leadership team.

Churches that are pursuing revitalization will want to start at least one new group every year. Also, before a group combines or ends, take time to pray and make plans to start another one. Carefully consider the target audience; doing so puts feet on your prayers, narrows your focus, fills in gaps, and assigns responsibility.

Identifying more sheep

Goals and plans are road maps to accomplish what God has sent us to do for Him. Setting goals to reach more sheep is a natural part of making disciples of all nations (see Matthew 28:19-20). Each group sets a God-sized annual goal for enrolling new people. The group spends time praying before setting the goal. Ask children, youth, and adults to offer goal input so they will take ownership of the goal.

After praying and setting goals, another important action is developing a prospect-care list. This is a list of people who do not attend a group. Group members share the names and contact information of friends, relatives, associates, and neighbors. This list can also include church members and worship attenders not enrolled in Sunday School. The list should have at least as many names as the number of people who attend the group each week.

After developing the list, planning for care and invitation are important. The group shares ideas about how to reach the people on the list. Fellowships, projects, and events are planned. The prospect-care leader assigns contacts that are made and reported weekly. The leader reports on goal progress monthly and provides encouragement and a challenge as needed.

Keep in mind that prospect care done irregularly is a poor expression of care. Contact should be made with each prospect at least every other week. Ongoing contact by the same person along with occasional contact by others often produces the best results. In *3D Sunday School*, David Francis says it may take an average of twenty contacts to lead a prospect to attend Sunday School.[1] Be persistent in your care.

Mobilizing the sheep

When the teacher tries to do the work alone, the span of care is limited. Adding member and prospect-care leaders increases care, but the best span of care happens when every group member is mobilized to care. What are some ways groups can mobilize care? Consider the following:

- Enlist and train member and prospect-care leaders.
- Assign absentee and prospect contacts weekly.
- Ask faithful group members to make ongoing contact with one assigned absentee and one prospect.
- Make multiple member and prospect contacts

prior to every group fellowship or project (using multiple contact methods).

- Provide a brief contact report and assignment time every Sunday prior to the lesson.

- Ask members quarterly to update their personal contact information (address, phone, and email).

- Ask members monthly to share names and contact information for new prospects.

- Plan periodic special events for making absentee and prospect visits or calls.

- Involve as many members as possible in planning fellowships and projects.

The more sheep that are mobilized for care, the richer the relationships will be inside and outside of class. When our love for each other reflects Christ's love, the class and church will be attractive. May Jesus be able to say of you that *"everyone will know that you are my disciples, if you love one another"* (John 13:35 CSB). May people be drawn to Him. May members be less likely to drop out. May prospects desire to know you better and come to your classes. May needs be met; my prayer is that the results will make you look more like the church in Acts 2. May you be *praising God and enjoying the favor of all the people. Every day the Lord added to their number those who were being saved* (Acts 2:47 CSB).

Where Do I Start?

Gather your group leaders. Pray together. Ask them to read this chapter. Then begin talking and working sequentially through the five key actions, one at a time. Seek input, ownership, and involvement in every step. Avoid doing this work alone. We are more effective together. Schedule monthly progress-report meetings. Check on progress, talk about next steps, adjust as necessary, and make assignments. And don't forget to celebrate what God is going to do!

Chapter 9

Worship Revitalization

Jason "Bubba" Stewart

O ur folks just aren't singing!" How I wish I had never heard that sentence.

My immediate reaction is to ask, "Why not?"

If I were to probe a little, I bet I would discover that at one time that church *did* sing. So, what happened to cause the reverse? I would look to see if the songs were written in a singable key or ask if the congregation even knew the songs. I would even go as far as to observe the musical accompaniment and equipment of the worship team and investigate if the congregants were competing with a sound system that is so loud it squelches even the most confident singer. But mostly I would want to see if someone in front of them is encouraging that congregation – big or small, country or urban, modern or traditional – to sing.

Pastors, do *you* sing? Your congregation will follow your

lead. You are their shepherd. The verb *sing* is repeated several times in both the Old Testament and New Testament as a command. But often when we conduct our weekly services, we find that our singing is poor, anemic, or nonexistent. Why is this? Why do we settle for lackluster worship? Are there things we can do to bolster our congregational singing? Are there ways to help our congregations engage with corporate worship? I have several encouragements for you.

I know there are different models and styles in the arena of congregational singing. I also know that for many years now, there has been a strong force and influence for equating certain styles of music with trying to reach certain segments of our communities. There have been many well-meaning pastors who tried to change their church's style of worship to help evangelize the lost. The problem is, their church may not have the necessary ingredients to make that change. If this is where you are, don't do it! Use what God has given you right there in your context. Yes, you might need to pray and search for key players, but I am certain that if it is a true need, God will provide. The following are some necessary elements to help revitalize your church's congregational worship.

Biblical Foundation and Direction

As a pastor, do you know why your congregation does what it does on Sunday mornings? Is there any rhyme or reason to your order of worship? I encourage you to include Scripture reading, corporate prayer, and a time of confession in your Sunday morning worship. We seem to know a lot about how to use our songs, our offertories, and our special music well, but if you want to have a biblical style of worship, you should include not only the preaching of the Word, but also times of confession, solitude, and prayer. Use Scripture as much as possible. You could even let children and youth read Scripture more often within your services (more about that later).

Musicians

There are hundreds of churches that don't have a single person to accompany the congregation on Sunday mornings – no piano, no guitar. The remaining options are to either sing a capella or use accompaniment tracks or videos. If you have a piano or guitar player, be very thankful for them, encourage them in their talents, and insist that they begin teaching others within the congregation to play as well. If you have a piano player, more than likely they play with printed music. If you would like your pianist to accompany a song that is not in the hymnal, you will need to find a source to print the music. Don't expect your pianist to pick up a guitar-chord chart and just start playing. Have you ever thrown a cat into water? How'd that turn out for you? One reliable source that I recommend is www.lifewayworship.com. You can find full arrangements that will fit your congregation, choir, and any accompanists you have.

If you find yourself lacking an accompanist, I encourage you to make it a matter of prayer not only for yourself but for your congregation as well. If you need a drummer, pray for one. If you need a guitarist, pray for one, and don't stop until God supplies that need. God may have someone in your congregation who already has a desire to play but needs some lessons. I would suggest that you as a church invest in that person and get them lessons. God may have blessed you with talent right where you are, but you have to open your eyes to see it.

Communication

If you have a music leader, instrumentalist, or singers already involved, then it's crucial to make sure everyone is on the same page and there is some sort of communication to help alleviate any potential headaches that uncertainty brings. You should not wait until Sunday morning to pick the hymns or the special music. Give your musicians the opportunity to bring their absolute best by giving time for personal rehearsal and spiritual reflection. Let your team of musicians know about future service plans and the role you desire them to play in those services.

A great resource to help organize your worship service – plan, order, timing, and all players – is www.planningcenteronline.com. This cloud-based management website allows you to stay connected to your volunteers and keeps them in the loop for when they are serving, what you would like them to do, and whether it be as a part of the choir, worship team, or something else.

Expectation

It still shocks me that many of our church worship and music ministries seem to have no rehearsal opportunity during the week. Many show up Sunday morning to do a quick run-though of the music and then wonder why it's a train wreck during the service. This will quickly frustrate a musician. Musicians truly want to do their best and do not mind rehearsing if it is a productive time of helping the team perform in unity. In fact, most musicians will find time during the week to practice and challenge themselves. But don't think for a second that any musician wants to be part of a poorly run rehearsal. The burden is, therefore, on the music leader to have their act together and know what needs to be accomplished in a weekly rehearsal. It isn't good to waste anybody's time; if you do, you will lose players. Trust me on that.

Sunday Service – Putting It All Together

Oftentimes, having a great corporate worship service depends on your ability to remove distractions. Those distractions can affect the congregation at the worst possible moment. Some examples of distractions are: misspelled words on the screen, the wrong introduction to the hymn, or even a microphone not being turned on. Other examples could be that a song is in the wrong key or the tempo is way off. When it comes to Sunday morning services, a little forethought and planning will go a long way. Think about things such as when "little Joe" is finished singing, where should he put his microphone? Or think about who will take the platform next. I'm not saying that every little cue must be written down or orchestrated, but it will certainly help the congregation avoid those "Wow, that sure was awkward" moments. We can alleviate many of those moments by simply thinking through the order of things.

Observe the engagement of your congregation. One tip I give to pastors is to set up a video camera facing the crowd. This could be off to the side or somewhere not too conspicuous. Then, record your congregation. I encourage leaders to watch the video later with the sound off. As you watch the video without the sound, you will quickly be able to assess the body language and attitudes of those in attendance. You will see whether they are engaged or not. It will be obvious.

As you evaluate music, I would encourage the pastor to begin asking questions such as:

Are we in the right key?

Are the tempos correct?

Have we even asked the congregation to sing?

Another tip I give pastors is to make sure each generation of those attending on Sunday mornings is included on the stage in one way or another. I encourage you to use children and youth to pray, read Scripture, sing solos, or anything you feel they could do. Get them involved and let their generation be represented. I also encourage our senior adults to be faithful and give testimonies to encourage the younger generations and to pray for the generations to follow. If we can accomplish all this, we will very quickly have a church with a multigenerational approach and mindset for its corporate worship.

One more tip I want to give. It's important to understand that thirty years ago, most of our church leadership were part of the "Greatest Generation." They survived the Great Depression and won (many times at a personal family loss) the great world wars. Their generation had a unique set of values concerning how churches should be and act. Emphasis was placed on dignity and respect, and thus the music of the church would follow.

But today, most of our church leaders grew up in the '60s and '70s and have no problem with drums or guitars in the church. What they do have a problem with is music that is horrible to the ears. My advice to those in music leadership is this: mix and mesh well. Do not let one voice or particular instrument have more prominence than another. Make sure the sound is well balanced and gives a strong accompaniment for the congregation to join in. Many smaller churches don't have the right space for a four-piece band. In that case, I would make sure that each instrument has a volume control and is wired through the sound system. With drums, I would suggest making the transition to electronic or consider using a cajón – a small box-like instrument – that can greatly cut down on decibels while still giving the important rhythm that is needed for many modern songs. By using the cajón, other instruments can keep their volume low as well.

In closing, I would highly recommend that as a pastor, you encourage your corporate worship to be multigenerational, biblical, and musical all at the same time. Make sure you utilize each generation as much as possible in your worship. Make sure you include biblical elements within the structure of your service orders. And please encourage the voices to be more prominent than any instrument on your stage.

I look forward to hearing you say one day, "Our congregational singing is at its very best!"

Chapter 10

The Art of Relationship Building

Dr. Paul R. Badgett

And I will show you an even better way.
(1 Corinthians 12:31 CSB)

O ne of the best examples of the importance of love relationships within the local church is found in the Bible. The
Bible offers the illustration of a problem church that is located
in a wicked city, the city of Corinth. The church at Corinth
had many of the same issues that churches face today. These
issues included divisions within the church, hero-worship of
church leaders, immorality among members, members bringing lawsuits against one another, marital issues, and the carnal
implementation of spiritual gifts.

The church at Corinth had been tremendously gifted by
God, and Paul acknowledges this in the first chapter of 1
Corinthians. The apostle says, *The testimony about Christ was
confirmed among you, so that you do not lack any spiritual gift*
(vv. 6-7 CSB). Paul was thankful that God had so gifted them;

however, they were misusing, in a carnal way, the giftedness that God so graciously bestowed on them. They were filled with pride as a result of the gifts they now possessed. They would practice one-upmanship. As an example, one church member might say, "I have the gift of speaking in unknown languages." Another, not wanting to be outdone, would then boastfully say, "You think that's something. God has given me the gift of healing." The church at Corinth had caused Paul great concern. He admonishes them:

> *Now here is what I am trying to say: All of you together are the one body of Christ, and each one of you is a separate and necessary part of it. Here is a list of some of the parts he has placed in his Church, which is his body:*
>
> *Apostles,*
> *Prophets—those who preach God's Word,*
> *Teachers,*
> *Those who do miracles,*
> *Those who have the gift of healing;*
> *Those who can help others,*
> *Those who can get others to work together,*
> *Those who speak in languages they have never learned.*
>
> *Is everyone an apostle? Of course not. Is everyone a preacher? No. Are all teachers? Does everyone have the power to do miracles? Can everyone heal the sick? Of course not. Does God give all of us the*

ability to speak in languages we've never learned?
Can just anyone understand and translate what
those are saying who have that gift of foreign speech?
No, but try your best to have the more important of
these gifts.

First, however, let me tell you about some-
thing else that is better than any of them!
(1 Corinthians 12:27-31 TLB)

Notice the statement Paul made above: *something else that is better.* What is he talking about? He is saying there is a way that is best when conducting the affairs of the local church. So, what is that best way? The answer is: loving relationships. Paul lays this out for his readers in chapter 13. He says speaking in unknown languages, preaching, biblical knowledge, and faith are all nothing without loving relationships. Charles Swindoll supports Paul's writings by stating, "Relationships need love. Congregations do too. What pastors need with their flocks is love, and flocks need it with their pastors."[1] Members of churches need to be in loving relationships with one another. Paul gives us fourteen different love-relationship imperatives in 1 Corinthians 13.

Love is patient.
Church leaders and members are to be patient with one another. William Barclay says, "The word [love] always refers to being patient with people, not with circumstances."[2] The old saying is true: "I am not what I ought to be, not what I am going to be, but praise God I am not what I used to be – God is still working

on me." Be patient with people. *But the fruit of the Spirit is . . . patience* (Galatians 5:22 CSB). *Preach the word; be ready in season and out of season; correct, rebuke, and encourage with great patience and teaching* (2 Timothy 4:2 CSB).

Love is kind.
The word *kind* means to be courteous, good, helpful, giving, and showering favor.[4] It means church members and leaders should reach out in kindness to others. Paul writes concerning the Christian life, *Be kind and compassionate to one another, forgiving one another, just as God also forgave you in Christ* (Ephesians 4:32 CSB).

Love does not envy.
Church members and leaders are not to be envious of what others in the congregation possess. They are not to be jealous of positions, friendships, popularity, possessions, or abilities. The right kind of relationships within the church always rejoice when others succeed and never begrudge the abilities of others. It has been said that a person often criticizes the one they secretly envy. The Bible says, *Let us not become conceited, provoking one another, envying one another* (Galatians 5:26 CSB).

Love is not boastful.
Church members and leaders do not brag. They do not brag about their buildings, baptisms, or budgets. Instead, they recognize, honor, and applaud others. It was said of the late Cliff Barrows, of Billy Graham-crusade fame, that he would never allow the focus of the attention to be placed on himself. He

always wanted the focus to be on others.[5] In the words of Dr. Thom Rainer, "This is not something taught in seminary."[6]

Love is not arrogant.

It has been humorously said, "Some preachers can strut sitting down!" A preacher that struts sitting down knows nothing about the *better way* to do church. A leader, pastor, or church member will be humble, modest, and recognize others ahead of himself or herself. Michael J. Gelb writes, "Humility is the soul of leadership." He continues his thought by quoting Nelson Mandela, former president of South Africa: "I stand before you not as a prophet, but a humble servant of you, the people."[7] The Bible says, *Therefore, whoever humbles himself like this child—this one is the greatest in the kingdom of heaven* (Matthew 18:4 CSB).

Love is not rude.

The church member and leader will treat others equally, with respect, and with honor. Dave Earley, author and online professor, shared the following story in a recent book:

"I used to have two colleagues who were similar in many respects but whose lives had vastly different impacts. Both had PhDs. Both were respected professors. Both were committed Christians. Yet one was very popular and loved by his students while the other was … let's just say he was not as well loved. The first man led a thriving ministry. The other man's church was dying.

What was the difference?

The way they treated people."[8]

Love is not self-seeking.

When seeking the *better way*, a church member and leader will seek to give to others and not seek for others to give to them. Paul writes, *No one is to seek his own good, but the good of the other person* (1 Corinthians 10:24 CSB). When a church and the leadership of the church focus on doing what is right only for themselves, it doesn't make a formula for revitalization, but it does make a formula for disaster.

Love is not irritable.

When a church and its leadership are seeking the *better way* to do church, they will not be quick-tempered. James Merritt once described many church members and pastors as being like a loaded shotgun with a hair trigger – the least little thing will set them off![9] The J. B. Phillips New Testament refers to these types of believers as being *touchy*.[10] The Bible says, *He who is slow to anger is better than the mighty, And he who rules his spirit than he who takes a city* (Proverbs 16:32 NKJV).

Love does not keep a record of wrongs.

Paul says that the *better way* doesn't keep a record of wrongs. A pastor and his church are willing to bury the hatchet and not leave the handle sticking out. They are not only able to forgive but also able to forget. Paul writes, *Do not repay anyone evil for evil* (Romans 12:17 CSB). A good example of this is found in the Old Testament where King Saul had wronged David. Saul had pursued David like a mad dog. Yet, when revenge was well in his grasp, David refrained and left justice to his God (see

1 Samuel 24). Sometimes the better way includes just letting some things go.

Love rejoices in truth.

The *better way* involves rejoicing when truth wins out. Love will not feed off tragedy. It will never take pleasure in the failure and shortcomings of others. The Bible says, *If someone is overtaken in any wrongdoing, you who are spiritual, restore such a person with a gentle spirit* (Galatians 6:1 CSB). A church or pastor will restore those who have failed; they will not rejoice at their failure. John Maxwell said, "Shoulders that bear [this] responsibility leave no room for chips."[11]

Love bears all things.

The *better way* to do church bears up under neglect, abuse, and ridicule. The Bible says we are to *put on compassion, kindness, humility, gentleness, and patience, bearing with one another and forgiving one another if anyone has a grievance against another* (Colossians 3:12-13 CSB). William MacDonald said, "The expression **bears all things** may mean that love patiently endures **all things**, or that it hides or conceals the faults of others ... love does not needlessly publicize the failures of others."[12] The Bible is clear: church members and leaders are to bear all things.

Love believes all things.

Church members and leaders are to always think the best of others. William Barclay says the believer is to be "completely trusting."[13] In an episode of *The Andy Griffith Show*, Opie was believed to have an imaginary friend by the name of Mr.

McBeevee. Mr. McBeevee was not imaginary at all, but a real person. However, Andy thought that Mr. McBeevee was Opie's pretend friend.

In one scene, Opie insisted that Mr. McBeevee was a real person, and pleaded with Sheriff Andy, "Pa, don't you believe me?"

Andy responded in an extremely tender way. "No, I don't believe in Mr. McBeevee, but Op, I do believe in you."[14]

The better way is to be completely trusting.

Love hopes all things.
William Barclay says of this verse, love "never ceases to hope."[15] The church member and pastor expect that good will triumph. The church member and pastor refuse to accept failure. Victory may seem impossible, but they expect to succeed in the end. The Bible says *we are more than conquerors through him who loved us* (Romans 8:37 CSB). William MacDonald says of this verse, "It is not simply that we triumph over these formidable forces, but that in doing so we bring glory to God, blessing to others, and good to ourselves. We make slaves out of our enemies and stepping stones out of our roadblocks."[16]

Love endures all things.
The word *endures* is a military term that means to be able to stand against the attack of the enemy.[17] A love relationship, then, is strong, and full of fortitude and fight. No matter what attacks a church member or leader, if in a proper love relationship, they will endure. First Corinthians 15:58 tells us to *be strong and immovable. Always work enthusiastically for the Lord, for you know that nothing you do for the Lord is ever useless* (NLT).

If you are a believer in the Lord Jesus Christ, then you need to be a person who understands the *better way*. The better way is to build love relationships within the body of Christ. Jesus exhorts us to do so. He said, *"Love one another. Just as I have loved you, you are also to love one another. By this everyone will know that you are my disciples, if you love one another"* (John 13:34-35 CSB).

The better way is superior. The Bible teaches us that faith is important and hope is important, but a love relationship is far more important. Why? It will last forever. Scripture says, *Love never ends*. It also says, *Now these three remain: faith, hope, and love—but the greatest of these is love* (1 Corinthians 13:8, 13 CSB).

Building love relationships will be worth the time and effort. A revitalized church will be a church that understands the apostle Paul's better way to do church. Relationships aren't taught in most seminaries but are vital to the health of the local church.

A common mantra in real estate is: location, location, location. In keeping with that mantra, there are three things you need to know about the local church: love relationships, love relationships, love relationships. Build relationships and learn the better way.

The intent of this chapter is to encourage you to take your relationships within the church to the next level. If you take your relationships to the next level, you will take your church to the next level.

Better Way Inventory[18]

Dr. Dave Earley, a licensed church consultant, says, "You can become the relationally effective person you desire to be."[19] Earley goes on to say, "Inspiration and information without application leads to frustration. But information with application produces application."[20]

On each of the following statements, answer with a number on a scale from 1 to 5, with 1 being the least true and 5 being the most true about your ministry. Respond as honestly as possible.

_____ I am patient with my fellow church members.

_____ I understand that patience is produced by the Spirit of God who indwells me as a believer.

_____ I understand that the Lord is still working on members of my congregation.

_____ I understand that my preaching is to be done with great patience.

_____ I try to outdo myself and other members of my church by showing kindness.

_____ I am courteous to the members of my church.

_____ I do not show favoritism to members of my church.

_____ I am not jealous of other pastors or other members of my church.

_____ I do not begrudge the abilities of other members of my church.

_____ I am not envious of the popularity of other leaders within my church.

_____ I do not consider myself a conceited person.

_____ I do not consider myself as being boastful.

_____ I do not brag about my baptisms, buildings, or budgets.

_____ I place others ahead of myself.

_____ I try not to be an arrogant person.

_____ I try to lead my church in humility.

_____ I understand the term *servant leader.*

_____ I try to treat members of my church with honor and respect.

_____ I seek the good of other people.

_____ I do not feel that I am a selfish person.

_____ I am in control of my temper.

_____ I do not consider myself as being "touchy" or easily irritated.

_____ I do not keep a record of wrongs done to me.

_____ I never seek revenge; I leave justice to the Lord.

_____ I never take pleasure in the failures and shortcomings of others.

_____ I have learned to bear up under abuse and ridicule.

_____ I tend to think the best of others.

_____ I tend to have a positive outlook for the future.

_____ I do believe that the believer will succeed in the end.

_____ I feel as though I can withstand attacks from the Enemy.

_____ I understand that love relationships are full of fortitude and fight.

_____ I do my work for the Lord enthusiastically.

_____ I know that nothing I do for the Lord will ever be useless.

Review your answers to each statement and look for the ones you marked with the lowest numbers. List below the areas you are confident the Lord would have you work on based on your inventory.

_____

_____

_____

_____

_____

_____

Now, brainstorm specific steps you can take to improve your love relationships, and write out a brief plan on how you will implement the steps below that specifically address your areas of greatest need for growth.

_____

_____

_____

_____

_____

_____

Chapter 11

Leveraging Celebrations

Dr. Paul R. Badgett

Many, O Lord my God, are thy wonderful works
which thou hast done, . . . if I would declare and
speak of them, they are more than can be numbered.
(Psalm 40:5 KJV)

One definition for *leveraging* is "to improve or enhance."[1] Therefore, to leverage celebrations in this context means to improve or enhance the work of the local church. Leveraging celebrations also becomes a tool in the hands of the pastor to aid in his work of evangelizing, discipling, fellowshipping, ministering, and worshiping.

The late Dr. Charles E. Stewart, former bi-vocational pastor of Rose Hill Baptist Church in Ashland, Kentucky, was once asked, "If you had anything to do over, after twenty-eight years of ministry at the same church, what would it be?"

He replied, "I would celebrate with my church more."[2]

What he meant was, the church had many wins during his

time as pastor, and if he had it to do over, he would celebrate more of them. When his church experienced a win, he wouldn't ignore it; he wouldn't just acknowledge it, but he would celebrate it. John Maxwell stated, "The true test of relationships is not only how loyal we are when friends fail, but how thrilled we are when they succeed."[3] A pastor who is interested in church health will be thrilled when members of his congregation succeed and will celebrate that success with the entire church.

We live in a 24-7 nonstop world. There are those who call it the "rat race." Pastors need to be careful because if they join the rat race, they might just become the rat. I believe this could possibly be true when it comes to celebrating wins. Sometimes the pastor can become so busy that he doesn't take time to stop and reflect on what is taking place in his church. It is so easy to offer a fist-bump approval for a win, head off to the pastor's office, and forget the success of a fellow church member. As a result, at least in the eyes of some, the pastor is a rat.

The Importance of Leveraging Wins

Why is it important to leverage wins? It is important because it may define the way others perceive the pastor as a leader. Celebrating wins may make the difference between failing or succeeding at a given church. All of God's people want to be valued and appreciated. When a pastor and his church fail to celebrate wins, there will be those who perceive they are not valued or appreciated. It's always good to remember that their perception is their reality.

The following are some reasons why a pastor and church should celebrate wins.

- Reminds members of why their work is important

- Helps members understand their role in sharing the good news

- Lets members know that the pastor noticed what they have done

- Leads members to feel they are part of the team

- Inspires members to set new goals for the future

- Reminds members that they are part of something special

- Becomes a morale builder

- Leads members to focus on the positive instead of the negative

- Reminds the church family that good things are happening within the church

- Builds momentum for the church

- Motivates church members to reach even greater goals in the future

- Provides positive energy for the congregation

- Helps build relationships

- Clears the way for the pastor and his congregation to reward church members who have gone beyond what is expected of them

A Strategy to Celebrate Wins

An internet article entitled "Why You Should Celebrate 'Wins' With Your Team" says:

> Some churches tend to be bad about celebrating wins with their team. This is probably because there is always so much to be done and so little time to accomplish our goals. We feel like we should just keep pressing forward. When we have a Kingdom mindset, we always feel the urge to do more.
>
> But if you never stop to celebrate the good things happening in your community, you run the risk of burn out – both for you and the other members of your team. Celebrating "wins" is a great way to pass the baton of ownership and vision, raise the level of energy and moral, and offer momentum to make progress to move forward.[4]

So, what is the strategy? Scott Wilson has developed a five-step strategy to help celebrate wins. This strategy is shared in the same internet article. It is as follows:

- **Story.** Wins should always be attached to a story. The article says, "Stories help 'wins' to feel more tangible and make them easy to communicate." It is important that wins have a name and a face. Attach a story.

- **Specific.** The church needs to celebrate specific instances. Instead of saying something like, "Things are going well with the women's ministry at the church," it would be better to say, "The church had more than one hundred women at the women's conference this past Saturday!"

- **Stats.** The article says, "When you communicate wins to your team or teach them to communicate wins to others, urge them to be specific. Tell them to say that there were seventy-three people who came to an event, not that there were 'a lot.' Including stats helps people to see tangible growth."

- **Strategic.** Wins should line up with the church's key values. For example, the church values children, and packing Operation Christmas Child boxes is a big deal at the church. This church exceeded their goal for the season. The church could celebrate by saying something like, "The church has exceeded its goal for Operation Christmas Child this season. We just want to celebrate with all those who had a part in packing boxes. If you packed a box, please stand!"

- **Short.** The article says, "Make sure that each win can be communicated quickly and succinctly, so that these stories can be shared over and over again." Hopefully, the church's wins will be shared by members through social media, at home, at sporting events, and even while waiting in the line at Walmart.

Things Worth Celebrating

Wins should not only be celebrated by the pastor of the church, but also the membership needs to be taught to celebrate wins with others. Everyone likes to win, and everyone likes a church that celebrates them. So, what would happen at a church that would be worth celebrating? The following is not an exhaustive list but might offer a few suggestions.

- Reaching a missions offering goal

- Completing a special-needs Vacation Bible School

- Starting a new Sunday School class

- Having a great turnout for "Trunk or Treat"

- Church staff anniversaries

- A new baby born into the church family

- Baptism

- Volunteers for the church nursery

- A great turnout for "Friend Day"

- Jesus' resurrection

- VBS professions of faith

- Birthdays and wedding anniversaries

- The completion of a building project

- Paying off the church's debt

- The purchase of a new church van

- The Lord's Supper

- Graduations

- New members

- Homecomings

- Mission trips

What the Bible Says about Celebration

The Word of God has much to say about celebration. Consider the following great illustrations:

> *Then King David was told, "The LORD has blessed*
> *Obed-edom's household and everything he has*
> *because of the Ark of God." So David went there and*
> *brought the Ark of God from the house of Obed-*
> *edom to the City of David with a great celebration.*
> *So David and all the people of Israel brought up the*
> *Ark of the LORD with shouts of joy and the blowing*
> *of rams' horns.* (2 Samuel 6:12, 15 NLT)

> *In every province and city, wherever the king's*
> *decree arrived, the Jews rejoiced and had a great cel-*
> *ebration and declared a public festival and holiday.*
> (Esther 8:17 NLT)

> *For the LORD has redeemed Israel from those too*
> *strong for them. They will come home and sing*
> *songs of joy on the heights of Jerusalem. They will*
> *be radiant because of the LORD's good gifts—the*
> *abundant crops of grain, new wine, and olive oil,*
> *and the healthy flocks and herds. Their life will be*

*like a watered garden, and all their sorrows will be
gone. The young women will dance for joy, and the
men—old and young—will join in the celebration.
I will turn their mourning into joy. I will comfort them and exchange their sorrow for rejoicing.*
(Jeremiah 31:11-13 NLT)

*Here is another message that came to me from the
Lord of Heaven's Armies. "This is what the Lord
of Heaven's Armies says: The traditional fasts and
times of mourning you have kept in early summer,
midsummer, autumn, and winter are now ended.
They will become festivals of joy and celebration
for the people of Judah. So love truth and peace."*
(Zechariah 8:18-19 NLT)

*It was now almost time for the Jewish Passover cel-
ebration, and many people from all over the country arrived in Jerusalem several days early so they
could go through the purification ceremony before
Passover began.* (John 11:55 NLT)

So, why should a church celebrate? The answer is found in the
Psalms. *Many, O Lord my God, are Your wonderful works
which You have done* (Psalm 40:5 NKJV). God is doing so many
wonderful things in His churches, and all those things ought
to be celebrated. Members of all ages should hear what God is
currently doing in their church.

How often should the church celebrate? One person sug-
gested that a church should celebrate at least twenty-five times

per year (large celebrations). However, a church should never limit the number of smaller celebrations throughout the entire year. Celebration draws a church family together. It helps to provide memories that will last for years to come. It provides an avenue to celebrate God's faithfulness in the midst of the family of God.

Revitalization and celebration go hand in hand. Real celebrations within the local church are worth the time and effort. Expend the effort to celebrate, and you will be glad you did.

Celebration Inventory

On each of the following statements, answer with a number on a scale from 1 to 5, with 1 being the least true and 5 being the most true about your ministry. Respond as honestly as possible.

_____ I am currently using celebrations in my church to assist me in the work of evangelism, discipleship, fellowship, and worship.

_____ I am thrilled when a member of my church succeeds.

_____ I celebrate with members of my church so they will know they are a vital part of the team.

_____ I celebrate with members of my church so they will know they are a vital part in sharing the good news of the gospel.

_____ I celebrate with members of my church so they know I noticed what they have done.

_____ I celebrate with members of my church so they know they are part of something special.

_____ I celebrate with members of my church in order to build morale.

_____ I celebrate with members of my church in order to focus on something positive.

_____ I celebrate with members of my church in order to build momentum.

_____ I celebrate with members of my church to recognize those who have gone above and beyond what has been expected.

As you carefully consider your answers to each statement, look for the statements you marked with the lowest numbers. List below the areas you are confident the Lord would have you work on.

_____

_____

_____

_____

_____

Now, brainstorm practical next steps you can take to improve on leveraging celebrations within your church.

_____

_____

_____

_____

_____

Chapter 12

Risk-Taking

Dr. Larry J. Purcell

A host of leadership writers have separated management from leadership. Management can be described as doing things right, while leadership can be described as doing the right things. A revitalization leader is not content with just managing a mess. In research that I led some years ago, it was observed that a pastoral search team would often paint a picture of the ideal church for a prospective pastor. The pastor would then arrive and find a church that did not resemble the picture painted for him. This isn't necessarily meant to deceive the prospective pastor.

In interviews with several pastoral search teams, I discovered that they were attempting to describe what they wanted at their church, rather than what they had. These search team members desired to serve a church by finding a new pastor whom they hoped could navigate them to this healthier idea of a church. But the honeymoon could end sooner for a pastor who sees a great chasm between what he was told and what he has uncovered. A pastor must accept that there is no perfect place and all situations or places have problems. The risk-taker must see these problems as opportunities.

Accepting Your Role in Risk

Risk is involved with all leadership positions; yet many leaders desire to avoid risk. I sensed God's call into ministry and knew He was calling me to be a pastor. I grew up in church and knew churches had problems at times, but the shock came when I observed both the manner in which church members reacted to conflict and their attitudes toward one another. Resistance of followers to change is the confusion of many leaders. In *Leading Change*, Harvard professor and researcher John Kotter writes about eight steps to effective change. Kotter identifies the first essential step as a sense of urgency.[1] A sense of urgency is the critical first concern of taking a risk. If you see the urgency and church members don't see it, they will not follow. If you see the urgency and they see it also, you will have more willing participants.

Developing a sense of urgency in your leadership team and the congregation must begin with the revitalization pastor. Risk-taking is the act of developing an unrest with where a church is because you see a better future. A revitalization pastor must not be content with the status quo. He realizes that what God used to bring a church to where it is today may not be what God uses to take the church where He wants it to be tomorrow.

Some leaders may sense they are not as well equipped by

personality to take risks. Risk-taking must not be restricted only to a pastor who thinks he has the correct personality for risk-taking or challenges. The Lord uses a variety of personalities in leadership positions as revealed throughout Scripture. Take time to examine the different personalities God used in the Bible, and see which Bible character and personality best reflects how you view yourself. How did the Lord use them, and how can the Lord use you?

The differences between Timothy and Titus are evident in the apostle Paul's letters. He issued a command to Titus: *The reason I left you in Crete was to set right what was left undone and, as I directed you, to appoint elders in every town* (Titus 1:5 CSB). Titus was on a mission to correct a situation that needed a rapid response. In contrast, Timothy received strong words of encouragement from the apostle Paul to continue as a pastor where he was. Paul wrote, *As I urged you when I went to Macedonia, remain in Ephesus so that you may instruct certain people* (1 Timothy 1:3 CSB). The biblical text demonstrates that both places were difficult. Both pastors had to accept challenges and take risks.

History is filled with the most unlikely people who become great leaders during times of conflict or need. The Great Man Theory states that certain men were born to accept positions of great leadership.[2] More often, what has been identified instead is that ordinary people have responded in times of great need or crisis. A revitalization pastor must not attempt to use excuses about why he cannot take on a challenge. The task of leading and developing leaders is a daunting one even when everything is going well; I'm guessing about this since I have never witnessed a leader accept a challenge where all goes perfectly as planned or anticipated. A false sense of urgency exhibits itself when a leader loses their passion because challenges arise. Leadership is demonstrated best when a leader, such as a revitalization pastor, faces obstacles.

You have probably heard it said, "If it were easy, everyone would do it." In other words, if leadership were easy, everyone would want to lead. Problems can provide opportunities for a revitalization pastor and leader to demonstrate commitment, build stronger relationships, and depend on the Lord's wisdom and grace.

David was an unlikely person to become king of Israel. A simple shepherd boy tending sheep who was smaller and younger than his brothers, David wasn't likely to achieve greatness in the minds of others, but he was called and equipped by God. David was ready for anything, whether facing the giant Goliath as a warrior or tending his father's sheep.

Understanding Your Personality

Personality inventories offer a variety of ways to study differences in people. The DiSC personality profile[3] identifies strengths and weaknesses of four personality types. This is a tool to help a leader better know himself and those on his team. Building a diverse team of leaders helps a revitalization pastor see the strengths, weaknesses, opportunities, and threats of taking any risks. God made you as a whole (body, soul, spirit), not as a part. However, it is helpful to examine the parts of your personality as they relate to becoming a better leader and risk-taker.

Every leader has a comfort zone that fits their psychological makeup or personality. The DiSC inventory is *not* used to determine the best personality. This tool can help a person better understand their strengths and weaknesses in leading and working with others. Leaders can use this tool as a means of building a diverse team of leaders. The more diverse a team is, the smarter the team; this is called "collective intelligence." When it comes to taking risks, I depend on people who are detailed, since I am not.

The DiSC assessment tool provides the following definitions for the four dimensions of the profile:

Dominance. Person places emphasis on accomplishing results, the bottom line, confidence. Concerned about task. Values the big picture but ignores details.

Influence. Person places emphasis on influencing or persuading others, openness, relationships. Concerned about relationships. Values people and unity.

Steadiness. Person places emphasis on cooperation, sincerity, dependability. Concerned about relationships. Values the team.

Conscientiousness. Person places emphasis on quality and accuracy, expertise, competency. Concerned about task. Values details.[4]

It is critical to understand that each person possesses traits of all of these personality dimensions. Each person has varying degrees of each trait, but one of these will be a dominant trait and another will be a secondary trait. Using the DiSC inventory will assist you as the leader in building a team or mentoring another leader. It is critical that a leader not think that they must be like someone they admire and have seen lead a significant change or take risks. Risk-taking begins with understanding your strengths and weaknesses and those of your team members. The diversity of perspectives and personalities helps a leader build the collective intelligence of a team. Recognizing the contribution of team members and valuing them strengthens a leader and team for taking risks. I have also used this tool in marriage conferences and counseling to help a husband and wife better understand areas of potential conflict.

Saying No to Status Quo

It is common for a church or any organization to be satisfied with the status quo. We are hardwired to be satisfied and seek the path of least resistance. Homeostasis is the point at which an organism adapts and stops changing. Organizations and people seek this sense of balance and comfort. A bodybuilder or athlete understands that the enemy of making progress in their sport is the refusal of new challenges.

Seeking stability and balance in a church can be observed when one change is effectively made and then the team or congregation declares it's time to stop. "We are good enough" is the feeling of some. All systems or organizations need to slow changes at times to allow the change to become a part of the culture.

An effective revitalization pastor understands that in the present technological world in which we live, change is a constant.

Seeking stability is not the enemy of urgency, but complacency is. False urgency can be masked by a lot of activity. A leader must not become content because of busyness. Activity is not necessarily a sign of life in a church or ministry. John Kotter writes, "True urgency focuses on critical issues, not agendas overstuffed with the important and trivial. True urgency is driven by a deep determination to win, not anxiety about losing."[5]

Risk-taking must come from true convictions about accomplishing the mission of our Lord. It is frustrating to see any sports team or athlete change their game plan from playing to win, to playing not to lose instead. This is where too many pastors and leaders live. The fear of failure or frustrations of past negative experiences prevent too many leaders from taking a necessary risk. The enemies of risk-taking will bring up how this did not work in the past, or how it will fail in the present. In a church or ministry, true urgency or risk-taking is driven by the conviction that we serve a Lord who deserves and expects the best from us. The title of a popular leadership book by Jim Collins, *Good to Great*, is a clear reference of why a revitalization pastor must not become satisfied with good.[6] Our Lord is a great God and deserves something great. Good is not good enough.

Chapter 13

Implementing Change

Dr. Larry J. Purcell

L eading change can be one of the best opportunities to develop younger and older leaders. The challenges you will face in implementing organizational changes can't be accomplished alone or in isolation. Change forces leaders to communicate and connect with established and prospective leaders. This chapter will seek to provide a skeletal outline for a leader to use in leading change and coaching a new ministry leader in implementing change.

Assess Readiness

A leader must assess the readiness for change in a church or ministry. Any established church or ministry can be resistant to change, even when its members say change is essential. Resisting change is a common experience of all organisms and organizations. Leaders must understand that even when a church says it knows that it may decline or die if it does not change, the readiness for change and the speed of change must be carefully assessed.

A leader that is new to any church or ministry will need to spend time in dialogue with leaders in the church and those most affected by a change. Communication is critical so that the leaders and membership know the *why*. Leaders will often express the *how* of a change, but until the leadership has buy-in to any changes, most will resist.

Early adapters to change are excited and hopeful, thus they can be ready to move quickly. Slow adapters are waiting to understand the why of a change or new initiative before moving forward. Many times, slow adapters will look to see who has early buy-in to a change before they make a move. Non-adapters may be resistant to any changes because of a variety of reasons. Some non-adapters just don't like change, while others may have had a bad experience. Implementing change requires a revitalization pastor to identify, as best as possible, each of these groups – early adapters, slow adapters, and non-adapters. Winning the support of critical leaders in the church and the early adapters will help move more of the slow adapters to support a new change.

Seeking a new vision for a church or ministry requires an understanding of the history of that church or ministry. It's important to communicate that the changes are not meant to suggest that what has been done in the past was not effective or good. Instead, it is a reminder that what God used to bring you to this point may not be what God will use to move you into the future.

Take time to look at the history and develop stories from this material when you preach, teach, or meet with various groups. A leader will most likely find the early, slow, and non-adapters in all classes and ministries. Visit a Sunday School class or a small-group Bible study. Visit with ministry teams. Call a town hall-style meeting, which allows a leader to build better relationships and hear concerns. It is a time to learn their stories as you help lead them to a better future.

Collect Data

Collecting data can be helpful to a new or experienced leader in seeing the spiritual and fiscal health of a church or ministry over the past decade or more. This data is critical in better understanding the context and culture of a community. If you're part of a larger organization of churches within your denomination, contacting a regional church consultant or a mission strategist can be a good beginning in accessing your demographics and reviewing your annual church-profile information. This information can help a leader better understand current and future realities as well as communicate this information to the various teams and the church members. It is critical that a change leader paints a picture of reality. It would be beneficial to have ministry leaders complete a study of their areas of ministry. This can be accomplished by having ministry teams meet to identify and list the strengths, weaknesses, opportunities, and threats (SWOT) of each current ministry. This can assist in building momentum to implement changes at various levels and involve more leaders in a new initiative.

Building a Change Team

Once a leader has a better picture of reality, he will need support from key leaders in the church. These key leaders may or may not carry titles. A key leader is someone of great influence in the church. The revitalization pastor needs to have the visible support of such leaders in building a stronger position for implementing change. Such a team may simply be advisers to a revitalization pastor, or they may be approved by the congregation as a vision team. In either case, the leader has increased his potential for support of the change and increased his collective IQ by involving others.

The change team will be key in demonstrating support for the new initiatives by publicly speaking to the changes and meeting with key groups or people who may be hesitant or resistant to change. These are key stakeholders who know the history of the church or ministry, including successes and failures. These key leaders will help you assess the spiritual vitality and emotional energy of the congregation for change. Timing will be a critical component to a new initiative. A leader wants to build upon success to gain momentum for his leadership and for future changes.

Building Team Spirit

Team cohesion is established around a clear, common, and compelling purpose. The team leader must ensure that all of the team, whether advisory for only the pastor or for a church-approved team, has buy-in to the changes. Identifying the roles of each team member provides a greater voice in the change process. The team leader's primary role is to assist in meetings to prevent only one voice from taking over and to involve all of the team. Team leadership encourages emotional commitment from the change-team members and seeks to build synergy among the team. Team members will provide expertise in specific roles such as finance, policies, or construction.

Vision Strategy

The change team will assist in forming a future-driven picture for the church to show them where the new changes will take the church. This will take a lot more time than many pastors are willing to invest. We live in an era of fast food, microwaves, and instant meals. Vision development takes time to ensure you are doing the right things. Once you begin a new initiative, it is very difficult to undo it – it's like trying to un-shred paper. This is a time to build greater change-team cohesion and emotional buy-in. In *Leading Change*, John Kotter wrote that a leader needs 75 percent commitment from his leadership.[1]

A word of caution. In Numbers 13, we have the story of the spies returning with a report for Moses and the nation of Israel. They had visual evidence of the land flowing with milk and honey. Of the spies who gave the report of the land promised by God, only two said they wanted to go forward. A congregation may not see all the benefits of a new initiative. The desire of most of humankind is to seek a place of comfort. A change leader and change team must be ready for a lot of questions and hesitation from a congregation. Team cohesion will assist the change team in overcoming many obstacles to a change initiative. It is during the many hours of discussion with the revitalization pastor or team leader that the team examines the areas of resistance. These valuable times increase team synergy and provide confidence to slow adapters.

Communication

As a pastor, your speaking often about the vision is critical to obtaining greater buy-in by the leadership and membership. Communicating change can be scary, but communicating a better picture of the future is essential. A host of writers on leadership and change emphasize the need to communicate often and in a variety of ways. A pastor can share during sermons, prayer requests, and in personal conversations with members. A change leader could go to small-group Bible study meetings, Sunday School classes, and ministry-team meetings to talk through the change. Technology is a great method of providing constant reminders of the change initiative through such avenues as PowerPoint presentations, a Facebook page, a church website, weekly bulletins or newsletters, and other means to make the new vision strategy a constant reminder. Having a short statement that fits on a T-shirt or baseball cap can be a constant reminder when the membership, sports teams, or ministry groups wear these during the year.

Transition

You have identified key leaders. You have shared your heart with the team. You have developed a clear, common, and compelling vision strategy, and you have been communicating that strategy to the membership. Now you should have momentum. This is a time of transition. Change is an event, while transition is psychological. A leader must understand the pull of culture.

Culture involves our beliefs, rituals, habits, traditions, and passions. Culture must be replaced, and transition is a critical aspect in understanding how this occurs. Just as gravity holds us to the earth by its pull, culture holds on to each of us by the familiar. You need enough momentum to move past the hold of culture, just as a rocket requires adequate thrust to get away from the pull of gravity.

Identifying Obstacles

You might think you are on your way, and then you begin hearing complaints or grumbling. In the book of Nehemiah, we first read about how Nehemiah prayerfully prepared for rebuilding the wall. Next, he toured around the wall and made a proper assessment of the situation. Then, he assembled the people of Jerusalem and offered the challenge of rebuilding the wall. When the rebuilding of the wall began, and even to the point of being finished, Nehemiah ran into obstacles. Identifying obstacles is critical for keeping your focus on the vision strategy and sustaining momentum. If you have not already done so, I suggest you read or reread the book of Nehemiah for inspiration. As you identify obstacles that slow or prevent the vision strategy, you need to remove these obstacles. Some examples of obstacles that may need to be restructured include the church's constitution and bylaws; some might also include redesigning the staffing and leadership paradigm.

As you make progress toward your vision strategy, it is critical to celebrate along the way. Saying thank-you to those who have given up comfort for a better future is essential. It is during these times of recognition and prayer that you can increase momentum. You may not silence those who are sure the change is not good, but you may win over more of the slow adapters.

Culture

You are almost there. The challenge now is developing a new culture in the church or ministry. The changes have occurred, but it takes a long time to make the changes a reality. You don't want to stop now. Recognize the changes and tie smaller changes to larger changes to keep the momentum going. You may need a short rest, but you do not want to give up. Paul states it well in his letter to the Corinthians: *Therefore, my dear brothers and sisters, be steadfast, immovable, always excelling in the Lord's work, because you know that your labor in the Lord is not in vain* (1 Corinthians 15:58 CSB).

Chapter 14

Leaning into Conflict

Alan Witham

When leading a church on a journey toward revitalization, leaders must lean into conflict when necessary so that the church isn't stymied in her ongoing journey of health and growth. While most leaders would agree with the need to lean into conflict when necessary, the reality is that most shy away from engaging it. The harmful tendency is to avoid the very thing that is essential to the health of the church. When the potential cost is counted (potential loss of people, loss of church income, decreased likeability by others, personal and family stress), leaders often opt out in favor of what is perceived to be an easier, less stressful route (not addressing it). As a result, the church suffers and the stress builds.

The Inevitability of Conflict

Great churches experience conflict. However, we can be

tempted to believe the exact opposite. We can be tempted to think, "Great churches don't experience what I am experiencing." We sometimes romanticize the early church in Acts or a growing church in another part of our state. We think, "If I were serving there, I wouldn't be dealing with the issues that I'm facing." When we study Scripture and study that growing church in another part of our state, we soon realize that great churches experience the same things we experience; they just navigate them in healthy ways.

If leaders are going to lead effectively toward revitalization, they must understand the inevitability of conflict in the revitalization journey. It is not a matter of *if* we experience it, but a matter of *how* we will respond *when* we experience it. Scripture has a great deal to say regarding the certainty of conflict. In Ephesians 6:11-13, we are reminded of the inevitability of conflict due to spiritual warfare: *Put on the whole armor of God, that you may be able to stand against the schemes of the devil. For we do not wrestle against flesh and blood, but against the rulers, against the authorities, against the cosmic powers over this present darkness, against the spiritual forces of evil in the heavenly places. Therefore take up the whole armor of God, that you may be able to withstand in the evil day, and having done all, to stand firm* (ESV).

On a spiritual level, pastors are engaged in conflict whether they like it or not. The opposition of the Enemy is expressed by three action verbs that summarize his strategy regarding us and the church: steal, kill, destroy (John 10:10). When we accept the call to lead a church, we find ourselves in the crosshairs of the Enemy. He does not want the church to grow. He does not want to see lost souls reached with the gospel. He does not want to see disciples developed. He is disgusted at the thought of personal, church-wide, and community gospel transformation.

Spiritual conflict occurs and heightens when we get serious about leading the church to storm the gates of hell within our communities. Therefore, we should not falsely believe that great churches don't experience conflict. The truth is that all great churches have and will experience conflict due to the reality of spiritual warfare.

Conflict often accompanies people's resistance to change. It is absurd to think we can continue doing things the same way we have always done them and expect things will materialize differently. Our sinful tendency is to prefer sameness or familiarity over needed change. In a world where things are so rapidly changing, the one place that some want to experience the "security of sameness" is in their church. Some say they want the church to grow, but deep down they don't want to change. When Jesus walked the earth, He was often met with opposition from religious leaders who wanted to demonize His actions and the changes He introduced. In Matthew 15:1-6, we read of Jesus confronting a group of scribes and Pharisees who criticized Him and His disciples for not ceremonially washing their hands before eating. Jesus confronted them by saying, *"Why do you break the commandment of God for the sake of your tradition?"* (v. 3 ESV). The scribes and Pharisees were holding on to things being the same as informed by their tradition; they could not accept the newness and change Jesus brought. Some people will cling to their idol of sameness, which is rooted in their love for tradition (or control). Then when needed changes are introduced, the result is conflict.

Conflict occurs when there are competing goals and agendas within the congregation. James proposed and answered a question regarding the source of conflict. In James 4:1 he asked, *What causes quarrels and fights among you? Is it not this, that your passions are at war within you?* (ESV). Someone once said that when you have two Baptists, you will have three opinions. Conflict occurs when people have a different view of how the church's present and future ministry should look. The danger is when those individual views become demands that their preference be heard and implemented "or else."

The pastor shoulders a weighty responsibility of leading people with different preferences, views, and opinions to recognize, agree, and engage in a common vision and preferred future that has been prayerfully received from God for His people. A healthy church is a congregation where personal preferences are considered secondary to what the leaders believe God is saying about His preferred future for the church. Getting to that destination often comes by way of conflict.

The Necessity of Leaning into Conflict

Great leaders who lead great churches lean into conflict when it is necessary. Just as we are often tempted to believe that great churches don't experience conflict, we are often tempted to believe that great leaders don't experience conflict. Do not think this chapter suggests that as a pastor you should be an autocratic bull-in-a-China-shop leader. When you lead a church, you are leading people. As a church leader, you must approach leadership with the mind of Christ, the wisdom of the Father, and the empowerment of the Holy Spirit to know when to lean in and engage in needed conflict. The provision that God gives you as a leader will help you navigate the tension between being a people pleaser and an autocratic bully, the tension between self-preservation (fear of man and being fired) and doing what is needed for the health of God's church, and the tension between moving too fast as a leader and moving too slow. Whom God calls (to revitalization), God equips (for revitalization).

Vance Havner once said, "A bulldog can whip a skunk, but it is not worth the fight."[1] There are times when leaning into conflict is not only worth it but also necessary. When are these times?

Leaning into conflict is necessary when identification of the current reality is required. There were seven churches referenced in chapters 2 and 3 of the book of Revelation. All of these churches received commendations and words of critical instruction from the Lord regarding their futures. God loved all of them (Revelation 3:19). The Father had a preferred future in mind for each of the seven. With all seven He led them to understand their current reality. Current reality is best summed up in the question, "How are we doing, *really*?"

We sometimes mistake current reality for how we think we are doing, but it is really about how the Lord thinks we are doing. The contrast between these two is best seen in the church of Laodicea to whom the Lord said, *"For you say, I am rich, I have prospered, and I need nothing, not realizing that you are wretched, pitiable, poor, blind, and naked"* (Revelation 3:17 ESV).

Their false view of themselves was a rosy picture. The Lord's view of them was a picture in black and white. A church must first recognize where they are before they understand where they need to go. Leaders must help the people in the church take off their rose-colored glasses and see themselves and their church in a black-and-white reality. Taking off the rose-colored glasses can lead to conflict, but it is worth it.

Leaning into conflict is necessary when difficult and controlling people have had a history of hijacking the church's future. Hijacking an airplane is a serious offense in our world. It involves overtaking an airplane by force and ordering it to go to a destination totally different from where the pilot and passengers intended. Hijacking occurs within churches when controlling people capture and take the church in the direction they want it to go, not in the direction that is best for the glory of God and the health of the church. Let's face it; some people don't want the church to grow. Growth, for some, would mean a loss of control and a loss of being able to call the shots. When new people arrive on the scene, those who have grown accustomed to keeping the church manageably small begin to lose influence and the ability to steer the plane in their hijacked direction; thus they create conflict. The conflict is never identified for what it really is. It is usually created over a side issue, usually directed toward the pastor or leader or the new people being reached.

People who hijack churches have been rightfully referred to as Mr. No, Mrs. No, or the No Family. When a great idea that could possibly lead to reaching people and future growth is presented, they respond with a resounding

"We tried that before," or

"That won't work here," or

"We are not going to do that."

All of these responses can be summarized in the single response, "No." When Mr. or Mrs. No are left to steer the church, they steer it into a tailspin. The apostle John confronted a Mr. No in 3 John 1:9. He proclaimed, *I have written something to the church, but Diotrephes, who likes to put himself first, does not acknowledge our authority* (ESV). Leaning into conflict is necessary to confront the potential stronghold of difficult and controlling people.

Leaning into conflict is necessary when a changing community calls for needed change within the church. Many churches struggle because they wake up one day realizing the church is in a community that changed drastically several years ago and they failed to change at all as a church. The struggling church often had a time in its history when it flourished. It was a time when people lived in the immediate area and walked or drove a short distance to church. Now those same churches have a few remaining members who drive to the church and don't live in the immediate community. A disconnect often occurs, and the remaining church members are not like the immediate community in age, ethnicity, or socioeconomic status. The change in the community often means going from once being monolithic (perhaps an all-white Anglo community) to now reflecting the diversity of other ethnic groups.

Conflict may occur when people in the church have a reluctance to reach people who are different from themselves. Leading the church to reach people unlike themselves may create conflict, but leaning into conflict is especially necessary when the truth of the Bible is being replaced with falsehood. Churches, like people, can experience spiritual stagnation that results in a lapse into spiritual decline and falsehood. People within the church can become influenced by the culture around them instead of being agents of change (salt and light) in the midst of the culture. In an unhealthy church, sinful beliefs and practices that mirror the culture can become accepted, and people in the church can find themselves in the quagmire of spiritual darkness and unhealth. In those instances, the preaching of the Word as the authority for the church's faith and practice may be met with opposition. Standing for biblical truth and confronting sin are often met with opposition, but the foundation of a healthy church must be the belief in the authority of Scripture and the belief that Scripture authoritatively informs all the church's faith and practice.

Leaning into conflict is necessary when people or families are at odds with each other. The work of revitalization is not one of just adding new programs and seeing greater growth. The work of revitalization is spiritual work. Healthy relationships (both with God and each other) form the soil from which greater health occurs in the church. Unforgiveness, bitterness, and resentment over present and past hurts poison the soil for church health and growth. Pastors often arrive at their new church with great hope and anticipation of the future, only to have their bubble burst when they observe the tension that exists within the church each Sunday because of broken and strained relationships and the presence of factions that may have existed for years. It would be easy to ignore the tension and pretend it doesn't exist, but the reality is still the same.

The pastor must fulfill the role of peacemaker and initiate a ministry of reconciliation. Jesus said, *"By this all people will know that you are my disciples, if you have love for one another"* (John 13:35 ESV). The challenge of the revitalization pastor is often summed up in this question: God, how do you want to use me to bring peace and reconciliation in the midst of broken and strained relationships within the church? Joining God in a ministry of reconciliation is not glamorous, but it is worth the work.

Leading through Conflict

When leading though conflict, it is necessary to practice, proclaim, and apply the truth of Scripture as conflict arises. Ephesians 4 is a great passage to which you can refer when leading through conflict. As revitalization leaders, we must lead people to be lovingly honest with each other. Ephesians 4:15 encourages us to *[speak] the truth in love* (ESV). As leaders, we must lead people to speak *to* each other, not *about* each other. Ephesians 4:25 says, *Let each one of you speak the truth with his neighbor* (ESV). We must avoid sinning in our anger. Ephesians 4:26-27 instructs us: *Be angry and do not sin; do not let the sun go down on your anger, and give no opportunity to the devil* (ESV).

We must think before we speak. Ephesians 4:29 states, *Let no corrupting talk come out of your mouths, but only such as is good for building up, as fits the occasion, that it may give grace to those who hear* (ESV). We must lead people to realize that navigating conflict is an opportunity to depict and proclaim the gospel. Ephesians 4:32 tells us to *be kind to one another, tenderhearted, forgiving one another, as God in Christ forgave you* (ESV).

Every conflict is another opportunity to practice, picture (depict), and proclaim the gospel. Christ Jesus leaned into the conflict of our sin and God's wrath and left heaven's glory to come to a people who were at enmity with Him. He died on a cross as an atoning sacrifice for our sin and was raised from the dead. We who deserved death and hell were offered grace and, thus, were reconciled to God through the death, burial, and resurrection of Christ and our faith and trust in Him. When we lean in, may we point people to Him!

Chapter 15

Lifelong Learners

Dr. Stephen C. Rice

W hat is a lifelong learner? Lifelong learning is the "use of both formal and informal learning opportunities throughout [one's life] … to foster the continuous development and improvement of the knowledge and skills needed for employment and personal fulfilment."[1] So a lifelong learner is a person who continually strives to gain knowledge. The Bible adds to our understanding of a lifelong learner. The word *Christian* is found three times in the New Testament, while the world *disciple* is found 267 times. *Disciple* comes from the Greek word *mathētēs*, which literally means "learner."[2] Simply put, a Christian disciple is a lifelong learner. I define a *disciple* as follows: A person who has come to Jesus for eternal life and has embarked upon the lifelong process of becoming like Jesus and following His leadership.

Being a lifelong leader does not happen automatically.

Granted, we all learn each day simply by observation and experience, but a disciple becomes intentional in their pursuit of becoming like Christ. The apostle Paul exhorts disciples to *be transformed by the renewal of your mind, that by testing you may discern what is the will of God, what is good and acceptable and perfect* (Romans 12:2 ESV). Intentional, continual learning is essential to any serious progress toward spiritual maturity. But how? How can we continue to learn throughout life? Here are six practical tips for becoming a lifelong learner:

Begin with the Bible.
As a runner, I read the best books, blogs, and articles that I can find about running. I listen to the best running podcasts available. I watch running-related YouTube channels constantly in my spare time. I even founded a Facebook group called Runners Helping Runners to personally learn more about running. Likewise, as a disciple, I read the best writings available so I can become a better disciple. Reading books is important, but reading God's Book takes precedence. No other writing can compare to the Bible because it is the very Word of God, and part of its purpose is to help us become better disciples.

> *All Scripture is breathed out by God and profit-*
> *able for teaching, for reproof, for correction, and*
> *for training in righteousness, that the man of God*
> *may be complete, equipped for every good work.*
> (2 Timothy 3:16-17 ESV)

Some people want to read the Bible, but they don't know where to start. When they thumb through the 66 books, 1,189 chapters,

23,214 verses, and roughly 622,700 words, they are overwhelmed. Here are some simple Bible reading tips that should help:

- **Read the Bible.** Don't make it complicated. You can literally start reading anywhere in the Bible and it will be helpful because God gave it to us for that purpose.

- **Read it through in a year.** A thorough, systematic reading through the entire Bible is a good way to attain a broader understanding. Numerous Bible-reading plans exist online and in print, along with many excellent Bible-reading apps.

- **Read it slowly during the year.** For several years in a row I read the entire Bible. The last few years, I have been enriched by reading smaller sections. I read slowly and often read through the same passage several times.

- **Listen to the Bible.** Apps allow a person to easily listen to the Bible being read while commuting, cooking, exercising, and just about anywhere you would want.

- **Read it with friends.** Go into any coffee shop throughout the day and you will likely see a group of people discussing the Bible with lattes in hand.

- **Read it with family.** Couples and families can benefit by reading together or by following the same plan and discussing their readings along the way.

Read helpful books.

As Dr. Purcell noted in the introduction, "all leaders are read-ers." A lifelong learner can benefit by having a reading goal along with a specific plan to reach the goal. Most reading goals focus on the number of books or the number of pages targeted for completion. Depending on your reading speed and avail-able time, you might adopt one of the following reading goals:

- One book per month (12 per year)

- One book per week (52 per year)

- One book per day (365 per year)

- One book per year (for those who dislike reading)

- One book before you die (for non-readers)

- Five pages per day (12 books per year based on 150-page books)

- Ten pages per day (24 books per year based on 150-page books)

- Fifteen pages per day (36 books per year based on 150-page books)

- Twenty pages per day (48 books per year based on 150-page books)

- Twenty-five pages per day (60 books per year based on 150-page books)

In addition to a goal, it is helpful to make a reading list or stack. I usually make both. I make a list of books that I plan to read throughout the year and place them on a shelf. I have other books that I might read throughout the year if time allows, but they are not a top reading priority. Throughout the year, new books are released that move into one of these two reading categories. Some readers are inspired by participating in Christian book clubs or by coordinating reading with friends or colleagues. Although it doesn't work for me, some listen to audio books as an effective method of learning and growth.

Use technology.

Technology can help lifelong learners mature as disciples. Christian podcasts and online sermons provide the listener with teaching from renowned leaders throughout the world. Bible study tools such as WordSearch Bible Online and Logos Bible Software allow a lifelong learner to access vast libraries and Bible study tools anywhere the internet is available.[3] Facebook groups along with apps such as GroupMe, WhatsApp, and Slack provide unlimited opportunities to learn and grow in virtual communities.[4] All of this is available to us on a phone or smart device. Often as I listen to someone preaching in person, I browse from the text to Bible study tools to read textual or background information on my phone that adds to my learning. We should use technology wisely to help us grow and learn.

Never waste a meal.

Relationships were important to Jesus, so a lifelong learner should give them priority. One of the easiest ways and times to develop and strengthen relationships is at mealtimes. Most people are going to eat three or more meals each day, so they should use some of those as connection points. It's hard to explain, but there's just something bonding about eating a meal together. Consider the following suggestions:

- Eat with family
- Eat with friends
- Eat with enemies
- Eat with fellow lifelong learners
- Eat with fellow church members
- Eat with coworkers
- Eat with those who need Christ

You can even combine mealtime with a Bible discussion or book chat to strengthen relationships and enhance lifelong learning. The unique combination of fellowship and food provides a healthy learning environment.

Get some exercise.

> *I have fought the good fight, I have finished the race, I have kept the faith. Henceforth there is laid up for me the crown of righteousness, which the Lord, the righteous judge, will award to me on that day, and not only to me but also to all who have loved his appearing.* (2 Timothy 4:7-8 ESV)

For years I've dreamed of running in the historic Boston Marathon. It is the world's oldest annual marathon and is often viewed as the pinnacle of the sport. In order to run in the race on Patriots' Day in April, a runner must first qualify by running a time on a Boston Qualifying (BQ) certified course that meets an age-graded standard.

In the fall of 2018, I decided on a BQ attempt at the Columbus Marathon in Ohio. Lee Staats, a running friend of mine, volunteered to run the race with me. He successfully qualified for Boston on two prior occasions and was excited about my potential to do so as well. Every marathoner knows there comes a point in the race when you question whether you can continue. During those race rough spots, nothing is more helpful than having a buddy running beside you. But for the purpose of a BQ, the only thing that matters is how quickly you *finish* the 26.2-mile course. It doesn't matter how fast you run portions of the race if you do not finish. You *must* complete the distance within the qualifying standards. The Christian life is a lot like a marathon. A lifelong learner should strive to run the race of life well and to completion.

The most infamous portion of the Boston Marathon course is called Heartbreak Hill. The hill only rises eighty vertical feet over a half-mile portion of the race, but the hill comes between miles 20 and 21, when the runners are often near exhaustion. Thousands of spectators gather there to cheer on the runners. During one race, a young man was near total exhaustion as he approached Heartbreak Hill. Halfway up the slope, an older man, in better shape, came alongside the younger man. He put his arm around him and quietly encouraged him. Together, step by step, they painstakingly climbed. The fitness level of the older man helped them both reach the top.

Exercise provides many benefits. You don't have to run; you can walk, hike, cycle, swim, lift weights, shoot hoops, or golf

– they all provide benefits. Exercise produces discipline and clear thinking. It helps you feel better, look better, and act better. Exercise even broadens your gospel prospect pool by bringing you into contact with others in your sport who need Christ.

Consider formal education.
I began my doctor of ministry program at the age of forty-three and finished at forty-six. We're never too old to learn. A person can complete almost any degree online all the way to the doctoral level. High-quality, fully accredited, formal education has never been more available. My doctoral studies benefited me more than any earlier study program because I was older and more mature. I had a better understanding and appreciation of the value of education in my forties than earlier in life.

Jesus deserves our best. Those we lead need our best. Become a lifelong learner!

Appendix

Seven Qualities of Revitalizing Prayer

God used Nehemiah mightily in a revitalization work. His life, therefore, provides a worthy example of the primacy of prayer in developing and sustaining a revitalization pastor. Please do not see the following as a list to be checked off but, rather, a resource to help you continue to grow and faithfully endure as a revitalization pastor.

Revitalizing prayer is driven by desperation; it is for the glory of God and the good of His people.

And they said to me, "The remnant there in the province who had survived the exile is in great trouble and shame. The wall of Jerusalem is broken down, and its gates are destroyed by fire." As soon as I heard these words I sat down and wept and mourned for days, and I continued fasting and praying before the God of heaven. (Nehemiah 1:3-4 ESV)

Declining or dying churches rob God of the glory due His name while depriving the community of a healthy gospel witness. Perhaps the most disturbing fact about the statistics frequently quoted on global lostness and declining churches is that they no longer drive us to tears. The shameful reality of the remnant of God's people drove Nehemiah to his knees and kept him on his face, fasting and crying out to God. Revitalizing prayer is characterized by this level of desperation for the glory of God and the good of His people.

- What about the current reality of God's people most troubles you? Where are they specifically missing out on God's best?

- What needs to change for Him to be glorified through your church in your community?

- What does the current level of desperation in your prayer life reveal about your active dependence on Him? Where might you be trying to lead from your own strength?

- What steps can you take to cultivate desperate, daily dependence in your prayer life?

Revitalizing prayer depends on the character of God.

And I said, "O LORD God of heaven, the great and awesome God who keeps covenant and steadfast love with those who love him and keep his commandments." (Nehemiah 1:5 ESV)

Our hope for revitalization is not based on our credentials as a leader or our collective capacity as a congregation but, rather, on the character of God. Many might scratch their heads wondering how a pastor called to First Baptist Church of Dry Bones Valley can pray so optimistically. We confidently pray for great and awesome things because we know we are praying to a great and awesome God.

It has rightly been said that the character of the Promiser is on the line in every promise He has made. If God couldn't or didn't keep His promises, both His goodness and His sovereignty would be in question. It is no surprise, then, that virtually all the great prayers recorded in Scripture begin by affirming the character of the One to whom we pray.

- What do you most need to be true of God in this season of life and ministry?

- As you labor to fulfill God's call, where might you be struggling to trust His character right now? (In times of discouragement many pastors can become disappointed and angry with the Lord.)

- What are some verses you can hide in your heart to remind you of His character?

- Spend a few moments adoring the Lord for who He is.

* * * *

Why Fast?

I continued fasting and praying before the God of heaven. (Nehemiah 1:4 ESV)

If we are to embrace Nehemiah as a biblical model for revitalizing prayer, then we must also be open to the biblical pattern of fasting.

We resist legalistic extremes, but why do so many pastors resist following the clear pattern of fasting that we see in Scripture?

When Jesus spoke about fasting, He didn't say *if* you fast, He said *when you fast* (Matthew 6:16 ESV). We are not surprised, then, to find that Nehemiah is just one more name in a Who's-Who list of notable biblical people known for fasting. There was also Moses, David, Elijah, Esther, Daniel, Anna, Paul, and Jesus Christ the incarnate Son of God. And then there were other people who fasted and were used mightily of God: Martin Luther, John Calvin, John Knox, John Wesley, Jonathan Edwards, David Brainerd, Charles Finney, and others.

As with all the spiritual disciplines, it is healthy to learn to walk before trying to run. Richard Foster's iconic work, *The Celebration of Discipline*, provides a comprehensive study of fasting and practical tips for getting started.[1]

David Mathis, author of *Habits of Grace: Enjoying Jesus through the Spiritual Disciplines*, has a great blog article called "Fasting for Beginners" that explains six suggestions for how to begin the habit.[2]

* * * *

Revitalizing prayer persists, interceding for the good of God's people.

"Let your ear be attentive and your eyes open, to hear the prayer of your servant that I now pray before you day and night for the people of Israel your servants." (Nehemiah 1:6 ESV)

Interceding is one of the key differences between leading, and leading spiritually. Nehemiah dedicated himself to persisting in intercessory prayer. The revitalization pastor persists in intercessory prayer, knowing that any visible victories that happen in the lives of the congregation have been won through the unseen battles fought in the leader's prayer closet.

> "A Christian community either lives by the intercessory prayers of its members for one another, or the community will be destroyed. I can no longer condemn or hate other Christians for whom I pray, no matter how much trouble they cause me. In intercessory prayer the face that may have been so strange and intolerable to me is transformed into the face of one for whom Christ died, the face of a pardoned sinner. That is a blessed discovery for the Christian who is beginning to offer intercessory prayers for others."[3] – Dietrich Bonhoeffer

- Do you have a plan for consistently praying for your people? Is the plan working?

- What do you most hope to see God do in the lives

of His people? How can you more consistently pray for these victories?

- Are your intercessory prayers for your people as frequent and fervent as when you first arrived at this church? If not, what might be hindering your prayers?

- Who are some people who have become almost "intolerable," as Bonhoeffer describes? Stop and pray that God would (a) help them come to repentance in any areas where they are outside His will; (b) love them through you, as our capacity for love is insufficient; and (c) grow your capacity for grace and long-suffering as you shepherd them.

- Do your people know what you are praying for them? Nehemiah, much like the apostle Paul and others, modeled the power of encouraging others by sharing the actual content of his prayers. There is power in sending a note or text letting people know, "This is what I prayed for you . . . ."

Revitalizing prayer revitalizes the pastor through the ongoing confession of sin.

"Confessing the sins of the people of Israel, which we have sinned against you. Even I and my father's house have sinned. We have acted very corruptly against you and have not kept the commandments,

the statutes, and the rules that you commanded
your servant Moses." (Nehemiah 1:6-7 ESV)

Tolerated or hidden sin is the greatest hindrance to revitalization. The broken walls and burned-out gates were painful reminders of the consequences of compromises that grew into rampant rebellion. There's no rebuilding without repentance. There's no turning a church around until the people are willing to repent and turn back to God, which must begin with the pastor.

Nehemiah owned his sin and personal responsibility for the plight of God's people. A revitalization pastor constantly comes before the Lord and confesses the sins of the congregation. The sooner these prayers turn from "them and they" to "we and us," the greater the hope of experiencing revitalization.

- The tragic, public falls of pastors invariably began as seemingly small compromises, rationalizations for "little sins" that were "no big deal." What compromises are you currently trying to hide in your life?

- Hidden sin is one of the greatest lies we tell ourselves. Is there anything you are trying to hide in your life right now that could jeopardize your testimony or ministry when made known? Is hiding this sin really worth giving up God's best?

- Pause now and confess your rationalizations and hidden sins to the Lord. Incorporate prayers such as Psalm 19:12-14 into your daily confessions. What are some safeguards that need to be built or strengthened in your life?

- Confessing our sins to one another is necessary for walking in integrity. Who are the people in your life you can trust to lovingly encourage you and hold you accountable? Prioritize building the same level of community for yourself that you preach for others.

- Pray for the other revitalization pastors in your cohort.

Revitalizing prayer depends on the promises of God.

"Remember the word that you commanded your servant Moses, saying, 'If you are unfaithful, I will scatter you among the peoples, but if you return to me and keep my commandments and do them, though your outcasts are in the uttermost parts of heaven, from there I will gather them and bring them to the place that I have chosen, to make my name dwell there.'" (Nehemiah 1:8-9 ESV)

The promises of God embody His preferred future for His people. This truth is why the majority of prayers recorded in Scripture are built upon reminding the Lord of His great promises. Of course, the Lord doesn't need reminding, but praying on the basis of promises builds our faith by reminding us of God's preferred future for His people.

"Christian prayer takes its stand on the solid ground of the revealed Word and has nothing to do with vague, self-seeking desires."[4]

– Dietrich Bonhoeffer

- What are some specific examples of where your church's current reality is the furthest from His promises? How can you incorporate the promises revealed in His Word into your prayers for His people? *Praying the Bible* by Donald Whitney and *Transforming Prayer* by Daniel Henderson are a couple of great books on praying God's Word.

- The revitalization pastor must prayerfully ask from time to time, "Am I leading His people toward His preferred future or just according to my preferences? Is what I'm promising living up to His promises?"

- Spend a few moments thanking God that *all the promises of God find their Yes in him* (2 Corinthians 1:20 ESV) and that He will ultimately fulfill them all in the lives of those who have put their trust in Him. List below some promises you are especially thankful for today.

Revitalizing prayer depends on the power of God to revitalize the people of God.

"They are your servants and your people, whom you have redeemed by your great power and by your strong hand. O LORD, let your ear be attentive to the prayer of your servant, and to the prayer

of your servants who delight to fear your name."
(Nehemiah 1:10-11 ESV)

The revitalization pastor often feels isolated and alone, but persisting in prayer revitalizes our confidence in the people of God. There is no indication in the first chapter of the book of Nehemiah that Nehemiah invited or called others to join him in his desperate prayers for revitalization. However, the longer he persisted in prayer, the more he was reminded that he was not alone. There was a remnant who loved the Lord and who were also faithfully praying for revitalization to happen.

The revitalization pastor needs to remember that the remnant has often faced greater hardships and made greater sacrifices for the sake of their local church than we can know. Do not mistake emotional exhaustion and spiritual fatigue for lack of interest or willingness. Revitalizing prayer reminds us that the Holy Spirit is still powerfully working in the lives of His people.

- Spend a few moments thanking God for His faithfulness to His people, for never abandoning you even in times of difficulty. Thank Him for the faithfulness of the remnant at your church.

- One of the first important steps toward revitalization is pulling together this praying remnant to bring focus to a united, concentrated prayer effort. What steps can you take to build or strengthen a revitalization prayer team, provide structure and direction to them, and equip and empower them to help lead the congregation in prayer?

- Take time to reflect and rejoice in the stories of faithfulness and kingdom sacrifices in your church's history. If you are not aware of these compelling stories, make it a priority to ask and listen frequently.

Knowing that celebrating what God has done in the past is one of the keys to revitalizing hope and commitment for what He wants to do in the future, how can you intentionally lead your church in celebrating His faithfulness?

Revitalizing prayer discerns God's timing; trust Him to open the right doors at the right time.

> *"Give success to your servant today, and grant him mercy in the sight of this man." Now I was cup-bearer to the king.* (Nehemiah 1:11 ESV)

> *Then the king said to me, "What are you requesting?" So I prayed to the God of heaven.* (Nehemiah 2:4 ESV)

Strategic patience is one of the greatest needs of the revitalization pastor. Everywhere he looks he sees so many things that need to be changed. Discerning the right timing requires diligence in prayer; otherwise, a visionary leader will risk running ahead of God. Nehemiah did not seek to create an opportunity, but trusted God to open the door at the right time. When God did grant him favor with the king, Nehemiah did not rush forward with his own preconceived plans. He prayed before answering the king. What did that look like? We do not know exactly, except that it fit the pattern of Nehemiah's life.

"We need not worry that this work will take up
too much of our time, for 'It takes no time, but it
occupies all our time.' It is not prayer in addition to
work, but prayer simultaneous with work. We precede, enfold, and follow all our work with prayer."[5]
– Richard Foster

- Are there any plans that you've been bringing to
  God asking Him to bless rather than seeking His
  plan and timing in prayer?

- Where might you need to exercise a little more
  strategic patience in leading change?

- How can you more intentionally model dependence
  on God through prayer among your leaders?

"There is a way of ordering our mental life on more
than one level at once. On one level we may be
thinking, discussing, seeing, calculating, meeting all the demands of external affairs. But deep
within, behind the scenes, at a profounder level, we
may also be in prayer and adoration, song and worship and a gentle receptiveness to divine breath-
ings."[6] – Thomas Kelly

These are just seven characteristics of revitalizing prayer that
are modeled in one of Nehemiah's prayers. What other qualities do you see in this or the other eight recorded prayers of
Nehemiah? Let's end by citing perhaps the most important one:
Revitalizing prayer directs all glory to God. In Nehemiah 2:8,

17-18, and other verses, Nehemiah was careful to acknowledge that the good hand of his God was upon him. May His hand equally be upon you.

About the Authors

Dr. Paul R. Badgett

Dr. Paul R. Badgett is a husband, father, former pastor, and currently a church revitalization consultant.

Dr. Alan Dodson

Dr. Alan Dodson is a husband to Amy and father to Allistair and Andrew, trained at Southern (from which he received the Francisco Preaching Award) and New Orleans Baptist seminaries, and currently serves as regional consultant for the South Region of the Kentucky Baptist Convention.

Rick Howerton

Rick Howerton is a church planter, pastor, church consultant, blogger, small-group expert, and has written or co-written multiple books. Rick's "Wise Counsel for Pastors and Church Leaders in about four minutes" seminars are available at www.kybaptist.org/stories/wise-counsel,3230. His blog posts are available at rickhowerton.wordpress.com.

Andy McDonald

Andy McDonald serves the Kentucky Baptist Convention as the North Central regional consultant.

Rob Patterson

Rob Patterson serves as evangelism team leader for the Kentucky Baptist Convention, is a passionate Christ-follower blessed by experiences of serving as revitalization pastor, international missionary, executive pastor, and is now helping churches reach Kentucky and the world for Christ.

Dr. Larry J. Purcell

Dr. Larry J Purcell earned a PhD in leadership, served as a professor at both the Southern Baptist Theological Seminary and the Southeastern Baptist Theological Seminary, and as a church pastor for over twenty years before coming to the Kentucky Baptist Convention as a church consultant.

Dr. Kenny Rager

Dr. Kenny Rager is an evangelism associate with the Kentucky Baptist Convention and has previously pastored three churches, one of which he planted with his family.

Dr. Stephen C. Rice

Dr. Stephen C. Rice is the team leader of the Church Consulting and Revitalization Team at the Kentucky Baptist Convention. Before coming to the KBC, he led four Kentucky Baptist churches to experience significant levels of revitalization.

Jason "Bubba" Stewart

Jason "Bubba" Stewart is the worship and music consultant for the Kentucky Baptist Convention. Before coming to the KBC, he led successful worship ministries within churches both big and small for over twenty-five years.

Alan Witham

Alan Witham has served as a senior pastor for nineteen years, leading three churches in revitalization. He served for twenty years as a consultant helping churches take steps that lead to greater health and revitalization.

Darryl Wilson

Darryl Wilson serves as Sunday School and discipleship consultant for the Kentucky Baptist Convention and is the author of *Disciple-Making Encounters: Revolutionary Sunday School* and of two blogs: sundayschoolrevolutionary.com and 28nineteen.com.

Endnotes

Introduction

1. *www.truman.edu/about/history/our-namesake/truman-quotes.*

2. Kouzes, James, and Barry Posner, *The Truth About Leadership: The No-Fads, Heart-of-the-Matter Facts You Need to Know* (San Francisco: Jossey-Bass, 2010), 5.

3. George Barna, *Leaders on Leadership* (Grand Rapids, MI: Baker Books, 1997), 17.

4. Church Consulting and Revitalization Team, "Revitalization Pastor Survey," Kentucky Baptist Convention, *www.kybaptist.org.*

5. Kouzes, James, and Barry Posner, *The Leadership Challenge* (San Francisco: Jossey-Bass, 2007), 31-33.

Chapter 1

1. See the appendix of this resource for a simple study of the characteristics of revitalizing prayer as seen in the life and leadership of Nehemiah.

2. Daniel Henderson, *Old Paths, New Power: Awakening Your Church through Prayer and the Ministry of the Word* (Chicago: Moody Publishers, 2016), Kindle Electronic Edition: Chapter 6.

3. The Church Consulting and Revitalization Team of the Kentucky Baptist Convention, *40 Days of Prayer: Devotional Guide for Church Revitalization* and *Strengthening Congregational Prayer, www.kybaptist.org/prayer.*

4. D. A. Carson, *A Call to Spiritual Reformation* (Grand Rapids: Baker Academic, 1992), 35.

5. Richard Foster, *Celebration of Discipline: The Path to Spiritual Growth* (New York: HarperCollins, 1998), 45.

Chapter 2

1. S. D. Gordon, *Quiet Talks on Prayer* (Uhrichsville, OH: Barbour Publishing, Inc., 2014), 5.

2. A quote sometimes attributed to Benjamin Franklin but is an adage of unknown origin, *www.quoteinvestigator.com/2018/07/08/plan*.

3. John Maxwell, *The 21 Indispensable Qualities of a Leader: Becoming the Person Others Will Want to Follow* (Nashville: Thomas Nelson, 1999), xi.

4. "40 Days of Prayer," *www.kybaptist.org/stories/40-days-of-prayer-devotional-guide-for-church-revitalization,620?*.

Chapter 3

1. E. M. Bounds, *Power through Prayer*, via Logos Bible app.

2. Will Mancini, *Church Unique: How Missional Leaders Cast Vision, Capture Culture, and Create Movement* (San Francisco: Jossey-Bass, 2008), 76.

Chapter 4

1. Benjamin Franklin included a version of this proverb in *Poor Richard's Almanack* in 1758.

2. *Secrets of the Dead*, "The Great Fire of Rome: Background," PBS, aired May 29, 2014, *www.pbs.org/wnet/secrets/great-fire-rome-background/1446*.

3. John MacArthur, "Church Leadership: A Study of Elders and Deacons: The Call to Lead the Church – Elders, Part 1," (Grace To You, 2020), *www.gty.org/library/study-guides/187/church-leadership-a-study-of-elders-and-deacons*.

4. The list is adapted from Terry Rials. Terry Rials, "Preaching Toward

Church Revitalization," *Church Revitalizer* (blog), January 9, 2017, *www.churchrevitalizer.com/preaching-toward-church-revitalization.*

Chapter 6

1. Ann Spangler and Lois Tverberg, *Sitting at the Feet of Rabbi Jesus: How the Jewishness of Jesus Can Transform Your Faith* (Grand Rapids: Zondervan, 2009), 14.

Chapter 8

1. David Francis, *3D Sunday School: A Three Dimensional Strategy to Help Members and Leaders Fulfill the Great Commission* (Nashville: LifeWay Press, 2006), 14.

Chapter 10

1. Charles R. Swindoll, *The Swindoll Study Bible* (Carol Stream, IL: Tyndale House, 2017), 1426.

2. William Barclay, *The Letters to the Corinthians* (Louisville, KY: Westminster John Knox Press, 2002), 133.

3. John Newton, *www.goodreads.com/ quotes/17247-i-am-no-what-i-ought-to-be-i-am.*

4. The Preacher's Outline & Sermon Bible *King James Version* (Chattanooga, TN: Leadership Ministries Worldwide, 1996), 164.

5. Cliff Barrows Memorial Service, www.*billygraham.org/CliffBarrows.*

6. Thom Rainer, "Four Steps to Church Revitalization Video Consultation," *www.revitalizedchurches.com/webinar-replay.*

7. Michael J. Gelb, *The Art of Connection* (Novato, CA: New World Library, 2017), 47.

8. Dave Earley, *14 Secrets to Better Relationships* (Uhrichsville, OH: Barbour Books, 2012), 69.

9. James Merritt, a sermon preached at Ridgecrest Conference Center during Sunday School week in the 1990s entitled, "Part of the Problem or Part of the Cure." From the author's sermon notes.

10. From 1 Corinthians 13:5-6 in *The New Testament in Modern English* by J. B. Phillips (1972).

11. John Maxwell, *Maxwell Leadership Bible* (Nashville: Thomas Nelson, 2007), 1457.

12. William MacDonald, *Believer's Bible Commentary* (Nashville: Thomas Nelson, 1995), 1796.

13. *The Preacher's Outline & Sermon Bible I & II Corinthians King James Version* (Chattanooga: Alpha-Omega Ministries, 1991), 166.

14. *The Andy Griffith Show*, Mr. McBeevee (TV Episode 1962), www.imdb.com.title/tt0512516. Oct. 01, 1962.

15. *The Preacher's Outline & Sermon Bible I & II Corinthians King James Version* (Chattanooga: Alpha-Omega Ministries, 1991), 166.

16. William MacDonald, *Believer's Bible Commentary* (Nashville: Thomas Nelson, 1990), 1714.

17. John MacArthur, *MacArthur New Testament Commentary: 1 Corinthians* (Chicago: Moody Press, 1984), 355.

18. The "Better Way Inventory" was used with permission from Dr. Dave Earley. Adapted for use in this book.

19. Earley, 248.

20. Earley, 249.

Chapter 11

1. American Heritage Dictionary of the English Language, Fifth Edition. Accessed April 16, 2020. *www.thefreedictionary.com/leveraging*.

2. Dr. Charles E. Stewart, in discussion with the author.

3. John Maxwell, *Maxwell Leadership Bible* (Nashville: Thomas Nelson, 2007), 1626.

4. "Why You Should Celebrate 'Wins' With Your Team," Vanderbloemen Blog, December 14, 2013, *www.vanderbloemen.com/blog/why-you-should-celebrate-wins-with-your-team*.

Chapter 12

1. John Kotter, *Leading Change* (Boston: Harvard Business Review Press, 2012), 23.

2. Gary Bredfeldt, *Great Leader, Great Teacher* (Chicago: Moody Publishers, 2006), 144.

3. See *www.discprofile.com*, or if you are interested in learning more about this tool, contact your KBC regional consultant.

4. Sugerman, Jeffery, Mark Scullard, and Emma Wilhelm, *The 8 Dimensions of Leadership: DiSC Strategies for Becoming a Better Leader* (San Francisco: Berrett-Koehler Publishers, 2011), 3-10. Statements about the DiSC profile used with written permission from DiscProfile™, a registered trademark of John Wiley & Sons, Inc. All rights reserved.

5. John Kotter, *A Sense of Urgency* (Boston: Harvard Business School Publishing, 2008), 6.

6. Jim Collins, *Good to Great* (New York: HarperCollins Publishers, 2001).

Chapter 13

1. John Kotter, *Leading Change* (Boston: Harvard Business Review Press, 2012), 23.

Chapter 14

1. Vance Havner, *Pepper 'n Salt* (Old Tappan, New Jersey: Fleming H. Revell Company, 1966), *library.melbac.org/books/vision/Pepper%20 and%20Salt.pdf*.

Chapter 15

1. Accessed April 17, 2020. *www.dictionary.com/browse/ lifelong-learning*.

2. Strong's Greek Lexicon (KJV). Accessed April 15, 2020. *www.blueletterbible.org//lang/lexicon/lexicon.cfm?Strongs=g3101&t=kjv*

3. WordSearch Bible Online, *app.wordsearchbible.com*; Logos Bible Software, *www.logos.com*.

4. GroupMe app, *groupme.com*; WhatsApp app, *www.whatsapp.com*; Slack app, *slack.com*.

Appendix

1. Richard J. Foster, *Celebration of Discipline: The Path to Spiritual Growth* (New York: Harper Collins, 1998).

2. David Mathis, "Fasting for Beginners," www.desiringgod.org/articles/fasting-for-beginners; Desiring God Blog, August 26, 2015.

3. Kelly, Geffrey B., and F. Burton Nelson, *The Cost of Moral Leadership: The Spirituality of Dietrich Bonhoeffer* (Grand Rapids, MI: Wm. B. Eerdmans Publishing, 2002), 167.

4. Dietrich Bonhoeffer, *Life Together and Prayerbook of the Bible* (Minneapolis, MN: First Fortress Press, 2005), 55.

5. Richard J. Foster, *Celebration of Discipline: The Path to Spiritual Growth* (New York: HarperCollins, 1998), 45.

6. Richard J. Foster, *Devotional Classics: Revised Edition: Selected Readings for Individuals and Groups* (New York: Harper Collins, 2005), 175.

Other Similar Titles

Disciple-Making Encounters, by Darryl H. Wilson.
ISBN: 978-1-62245-464-8

Dying to Grow, by Nathan Lorick.
ISBN: 978-1-62245-107-4

Return to the Margins, by Terry Coy.
ISBN: 978-1-62245-229-3

It's a God Thing, by Charles L. Roesel.
ISBN: 978-1-62245-148-7

The Soul Winner, by Charles H. Spurgeon.
ISBN: 978-1-62245-284-2

The Ministry of Intercession, by Andrew Murray.
ISBN: 978-1-62245-339-9

Prevailing Prayer, by Dwight L. Moody.
ISBN: 978-1-62245-567-6

Words of Counsel, by Charles H. Spurgeon.
ISBN: 978-1-62245-502-7

How to Bring Men to Christ, by Reuben A. Torrey.
ISBN: 978-1-62245-613-0

The Greatest Fight, by Charles H. Spurgeon.
ISBN: 978-1-62245-504-1

A Word to Fellow Pastors and Other Christian Leaders,
by Horatius Bonar. ISBN: 978-1-62245-619-2

Pastor and Prayer, by E. M. Bounds.
ISBN: 978-1-62245-575-1

How to Promote and Conduct a Successful Revival,
by Reuben A. Torrey. ISBN: 978-1-62245-667-3

Evangelism, by G. Campbell Morgan.
ISBN: 978-1-62245-547-8

Made in United States
North Haven, CT
11 November 2022

26568739R00112